A CREATIVE STEP-BY-STEP GUIDE TO

HANGING BASKETS
AND WALL CONTAINERS

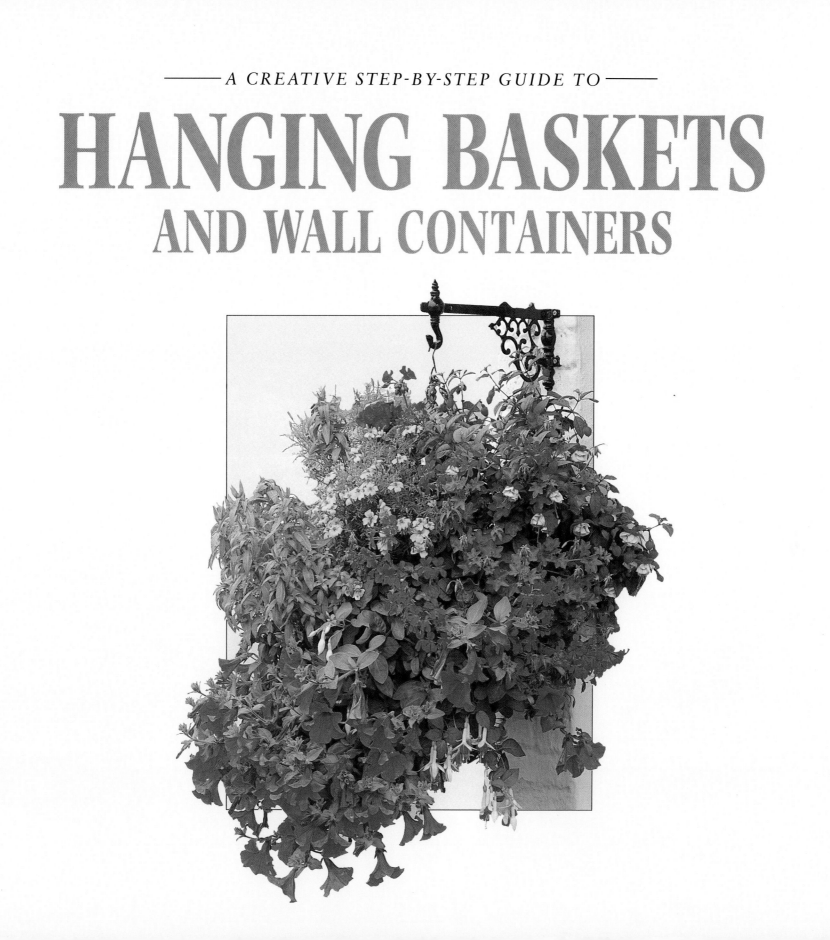

A CREATIVE STEP-BY-STEP GUIDE TO

HANGING BASKETS
AND WALL CONTAINERS

Author
Jenny Hendy

Photographer
Neil Sutherland

AURA

4663
This edition published in 1998 by Aura Books
Copyright © 1996 Quadrillion Publishing Ltd.,
Godalming Business Centre, Woolsack Way,
Godalming, Surrey, England. GU7 1XW
Printed and bound in Singapore
ISBN 0-94779-311-9

Credits
Edited and designed: Ideas into Print
Photographs: Neil Sutherland
Typesetting: Ideas into Print and Ash Setting and Printing
Production Director: Gerald Hughes
Production: Ruth Arthur, Sally Connolly, Neil Randles,
Karen Staff, Jonathan Tickner

THE AUTHOR

Jenny Hendy has always been excited by plants and
gardening and by the time she started school was already
entering horticultural competitions! Despite field trips
blighted by hay fever, she went on to study for and
complete an honors degree in botany at the University
College of North Wales, Bangor. Her first job after
graduation was in a garden center, where she gained
practical experience of the trade. In 1985 she joined the
staff of Gardening Which? magazine, part of the
Consumers' Association, and began researching and
writing gardening articles, concentrating on ornamental
plants and garden design. It was then that her interest in
container gardening really took off. A year later, she took
time out to join a French expedition to South America,
realizing a long-held ambition to explore the rainforest.
Now a freelance journalist, she divides her time between
books and magazines, as well as giving lectures and
demonstrations. She and her husband Chris are busy
working together on their third garden, designed,
constructed and planted from scratch, a labor of love for
which, like every gardener, she wishes she had more time!

THE PHOTOGRAPHER

Neil Sutherland has more than 25 years experience in a
wide range of photographic fields, including still-life,
portraiture, reportage, natural history, cookery, landscape
and travel. His work has been published in countless books
and magazines throughout the world.

Half-title page: A superb, well-tended hanging basket.
Title page: Tiny silver baskets make a delightful gift.
Copyright page: A fine basket in harmony with the house.

CONTENTS

Narcissus
'Tête-à-Tête'
(dwarf daffodil)

Hardy hybrid
primrose

Anemone blanda
(windflower)

Hedera helix
'Sagittifolia Variegata'
(variegated ivy)

Erica x darleyensis
'Silberschmelze' syn
'Molten Silver'
(heather)

Arabis alpina
caucasica variety
(pink arabis)

10

MAKING THE MOST OF HANGING BASKETS

Hanging baskets and wall pots allow you to cultivate what is to all intents and purposes a hostile environment - the wall of a house is like a sheer cliff face with no toeholds! But fix in a few screws, hooks and brackets and you can transform bare bricks into luxuriant hanging gardens.

The wonderful thing about baskets is that the display is only temporary. You can ring the changes from year to year and from season to season and have great fun experimenting with different plants and color schemes. Go ahead and break some gardening rules! Mix alpines with bedding plants, houseplants with herbs, and shrubs with tender perennials - you will be surprised at how good the results can be. Once you branch out into using plants other than those traditionally associated with baskets, the palette of colors and textures available increases enormously. Baskets and wall pots are available in a wide range of materials and designs, some more practical than others. On the following pages you will find advice on lining and hanging up baskets, both indoors and outside.

There is no need to keep buying new baskets. As this book shows, you can recycle the same container through the seasons, using a variety of colors and plant associations to produce strikingly different results each time. Generally speaking, hanging baskets are a feature of the summer garden only, but this certainly does not have to be the case. This book takes you through the seasons, with ideas on what plants are available at the time and where to locate them in the garden center. Even in the depths of winter, you can enjoy wonderful displays of fresh flowers, colorful berries and foliage around the door.

Left: A basket of spring flowers and bulbs. Right: A wall basket of trailing geraniums and variegated felicia.

The new trailing petunia variety Surfinia 'Blue Vein'.

Where and how to hang your basket

Practicality and safety, aesthetics and the needs of your plants are the points to bear in mind when hanging a basket. Do not hang it where people will knock their heads on it, or so close to the door that you must fight your way through trailing foliage to get in and out; remember, baskets can grow considerably bigger than when first planted! Where space is limited, consider wall pots and baskets as a space-saving alternative. You need not always hang them from traditional brackets, either. On a pergola or porch, all you need to do is to screw sturdy hooks into the woodwork. Custom-built wall baskets usually come with screw holes, but you can fix ordinary round plants pots to the wall or drainpipes using specially designed clips. Where you position baskets can make all the difference to how easy they are to maintain and how well the plants perform. Baskets need almost daily attention - feeding, watering, deadheading - so hang them for easy access or fit pulleys for raising and lowering. Keep plants with similar requirements for light and moisture together, so that you can hang them where they will have the optimum conditions for growth.

Above: *Trailing plants need plenty of space. Single-subject baskets such as this cascading petunia can be very effective, but must be grown to perfection, as there are no other plants to distract the eye.*

Right: *These cleverly designed coach lamps have hooks on which you can suspend hanging baskets. At night, the flowers will be illuminated, making a real welcome for visitors.*

Left: A symmetrically planted wall basket on a central pillar between two doorways emphasizes the architectural detail perfectly. The verbena, petunia and variegated felicia in this basket all prefer a sunny position - only the tuberous begonias and ivy are tolerant of shade. In this case, a spot in good light out of strong midday sun would be ideal.

Fixing a bracket to a wall

Once filled with potting mixture and plants, hanging baskets can be surprisingly heavy, so it is important to fix the brackets properly. When attaching a bracket, you need to plug the hole to prevent the screw from working its way out (see below). Always use the correct size bracket for the basket. These are usually sold for a particular basket diameter, for example 12in(30cm), 14in(35cm), etc.

Left: Put the bracket against the wall and mark the position of the screw holes using a felt-tipped pen. Using a hammer-action drill and the correct sized masonry drill bit, drill the top hole.

Left: Push the wall plug into the hole and then put the bracket back in place. Fix the top screw loosely so that you can check the position of the second hole. Make any necessary adjustments.

Below: The traditional way to hang baskets is from a bracket fixed to a wall or fence. Brackets are available in many designs, some simple, some highly ornamental.

Right: Drill and plug the second hole and screw the bracket firmly in place. For fixing wall pots and baskets directly to a wall, follow the same steps for drilling and plugging.

Feeding and watering

Watering should be a daily or, better still, twice daily routine, especially for baskets in full sun or in a windy spot. Never rely on rainfall to do the job for you and do not wait for plants to wilt before attending to them. Some basket plants never fully recover and soilless compost is notoriously difficult to rewet once it has dried beyond a certain point. Luckily, there are several ways to make the job easier. You can buy easy-reach attachments for hose pipes and devices that allow you to raise or lower a basket for maintenance. The trick is to apply a slow, steady stream of water that has a real chance of soaking in. Do not assume that just because water starts running out, the basket has reached capacity. It is more effective to water several times through the day, using a small watering can, than to give baskets a quick deluge that inevitably results in the water pouring straight out. Use 14- or 16in(35 or 40cm) diameter baskets, rather than 12in(30cm) ones, unless you can guarantee adequate watering, and choose self-watering baskets if you are unable to water daily in summer. Once the feed in the potting mix has been used up (see back of bag for timings), begin to apply liquid feeds, usually once a week at full strength or every time you water, using roughly half the recommended dose. Too much leafy growth at the expense of flowers usually means that you are using a product with too high a proportion of nitrogen. Choose a fertilizer for bedding and other flowering plants. A slow-release fertilizer applied at the beginning of the season makes the job even easier.

Feeding your plants

Regular liquid feeding gives the best results, but if you do not have the time or are apt to forget, use slow-release feeding pellets or tablets. Insert these into the potting mix at planting time. They last the whole season, releasing feed when plants are watered. The amount varies according to the temperature.

A perforated plate covered with capillary matting separates the potting mixture from the reservoir.

Watering tube for filling reservoir.

A capillary matting wick draws the water up from the reservoir to the potting mixture.

Self-watering hanging baskets have a hidden reservoir of water below the potting mix.

Left: *A plastic bottle cut in half, the pointed end buried in the soil at planting time, becomes a mini-reservoir that is soon hidden by the growing plants.*

Right: *Special long-lance attachments that fit onto a hose pipe allow you to reach up into high baskets. Using the on-off switch on the handle, you can deliver the water in small doses.*

Right: An empty plastic bottle is also a useful aid to watering, especially if you just have one or two baskets. It is much lighter than a full watering can and is therefore ideal for overhead watering.

Above: *Easy-to-operate pulley systems clip onto the hanging hook or bracket and give access to baskets for feeding, watering and maintenance.*

Above: *Reach up to the base of the basket and pull it down to attend to plants. Nudge the basket up to release the lock and push it back into place.*

Soaking a dried out hanging basket

1 *Peat-based potting mix is very difficult to rewet if a basket has dried out. Water just tends to run straight through. If this happens, fill a sink or bowl with water and add a drop of liquid detergent to help the water 'stick' to the soil.*

2 *Plunge the basket into the water and leave it until the potting mix is completely saturated. Allow the basket to drain, then stand it in a sheltered, shady place until the plants recover. Cut off dead shoots and flowers before rehanging.*

Maintaining your basket while you are away

The best solution to the problem of how to look after hanging baskets is a willing neighbor, but if you cannot arrange for someone to stand in for you until your return, then you will need to make other provisions. First, soak the baskets so that the soil is saturated with water and then put them down in a shady spot at floor level. Up on the wall they are much more exposed to drying elements - wind, sun and heat radiated back onto the basket from the wall. This procedure should keep baskets in reasonable condition for three or four days unless the weather is exceptionally hot. Even if someone is coming in to water, it is a good idea to do this, clustering the baskets together in one place for easy access. For longer periods, a little more preparation is required. 'Planting' baskets in a shady border is a good solution for maintaining traditional baskets lined with moss or another porous material, as moisture loss is dramatically reduced when the sides of the basket are surrounded by damp soil. Another technique is to set up some kind of automatic watering system, such as the capillary wick method, which is ideal for wall pots and baskets with solid sides. You can of course combine the two methods for traditional baskets. Whichever method you choose, be sure to remove flowers that will be over by your return and deal with any pest problems before you leave.

A capillary wick

A couple of days before leaving, cut a piece of capillary matting into a long strip. Soak it, push one end into the basket and leave the other end in water. Check that the plants take up the water.

1 *Find a spot in a sheltered, shady part of the garden and dig a hole large enough to accommodate the base of the basket up to planting level.*

2 *Water the hole thoroughly and soak the basket in readiness for planting. You must ensure maximum saturation before you go away.*

3 *Sprinkle a few slug pellets into and around the hole and in the top of the basket to protect against attack. Check for slugs on your return.*

5 *Drastic though it may seem, you must remove all the flowers. Bunch together the stems of small-flowered plants and cut them back near the base.*

6 *Take off any blooms that have just started to open and would be over on your return. Water the basket and surrounding soil once more.*

4 *Lifting trailers clear of the base, lower the basket into the prepared hole. Rest the hanging chain on the surface and then backfill with soil.*

Baskets sunk into damp soil and surrounded by plants in a shady border lose water much less rapidly than if left on a wall.

A backdrop for the basket

The success of any hanging basket display is closely tied in with the backdrop you select. Backgrounds can be neutral in color, complementary or contrasting. You can hang most baskets against white-washed or light pastel-colored rendering and woodwork, gray stone or weathered fencing. Brickwork is more tricky; there are so many colors and orange-red makes a particularly difficult backdrop, especially for certain pink flower shades. In this case, it is best to stick to other 'hot' colors - flame reds, oranges and golden yellows - or contrasting 'cool' silver-grays, blues, purples and white. These hot and cool colors also work well when mixed together. Another alternative for difficult or unattractive backdrops is to create your own. Fix trellis panels to the wall, paint or stain them an appropriate color, then fix brackets above or through the panels so that the flowers and foliage hang down over the new backdrop.

Some of the strongest visual effects come from linking the color of basket plants to a color used in the background, say an attractively colored front door or window shutters. Complement white-washed walls and woodwork with mixed baskets of silver, blue, lilac and white or contrast blue paintwork with yellow, orange, cerise-pink or red schemes. Plain greenery makes an ideal foil for colorful mixed baskets and it is well worth fixing hanging baskets onto climber-clad walls and fences. If the foliage backdrop is variegated, pick strong colors and bold foliage so that the basket really stands out. For a more subtle effect, try matching or toning basket plants with the flowers of a climber or wall shrub.

Above: Salmon-pink geraniums, busy Lizzie and blue lobelia are perfectly complemented by a pale brick backdrop. The scheme would not work so well against a red-brick wall.

Left: Baskets can look beautiful hung on a climber-clad wall, all the more so when the flowers and foliage of the backdrop match the basket color scheme. Here lilac-pink impatiens team up with purple clematis.

Above: *Without a basket, this white-washed wall could have looked rather dull until the pyracantha berries developed their color in early fall.*

Left: *Here, matching arrangements of cherry-red trailing begonias, blue lobelia and lime-green lysimachia make a strong contrast to a starkly painted black-and-white entrance.*

Tuberous begonias and trailing lobelia are happy in a shady spot.

Making an impact with baskets

No matter how tiny a backyard you have, there will always be space for hanging baskets. Even if the ground is paved, bare walls and fences can be instantly transformed into a hanging garden. In a new plot, where climbers and wall shrubs are still very small, trailing foliage from hanging baskets can cover the gaps easily and basket blooms provide a continuation of color from the border up. Baskets and wall pots can also be used to draw the eye towards an attractive feature, such as a house nameplate or decorative window. There are a number of ways to make such vertical displays even more eye-catching. Hang an identical basket on either side of a doorway and straight away you have doubled the dramatic effect. If two or three baskets are grouped very close to one another, you can persuade people into thinking that it is just one enormous arrangement. And, with several baskets hanging in a line, it is possible to create a continuous ribbon of color. This technique is all the more effective if the basket plants are chosen to fit into a particular color scheme or if an identical variety is used throughout. (Pick a reliable variety, such as Swiss balcony geraniums.) You can strengthen the design further by mirroring the planting in windowboxes, pots and planters in the rest of the garden. A variation on this theme is to hang baskets between windowboxes, forming an unbroken line of flowers.

For an informal look and to cover a large area, such as a featureless house or garage wall, stagger the baskets at different heights. Cluster groups of very small wall pots together and 'anchor' them visually with one large basket.

Left: *Ivy-leaved geraniums (Pelargonium), verbena and diascia in rich pinks and reds contrast with deep blue lobelia in these matching baskets. Hung side by side, the plants grow and merge together, forming what looks at first like a single large basket, perfectly in scale with the surrounding architecture.*

Right: Simple color schemes often create the strongest impact. Here, vibrant red trailing geraniums contrast with the pale stone and blue paintwork to form a band of flowers across the front of the house. The same color is used for the troughs and planters below.

Above: Here, color is brought right up to the front door by filling the gaps at the end of the window troughs with hanging baskets at the same level.

Left: Hanging baskets provide extra growing space in this small patio garden. The baskets are an integral part of the scheme and, with other climbers and wall plants, create a colorful facade for the fencing.

Right: The eye is immediately drawn to this charming cottage-style window surrounded by the lush foliage of a vine, Vitis coignetiae, and flowers from the hanging baskets. On one side is a cluster of matching wall pots filled with yellow-flowered creeping Jenny (Lysimachia nummularia). In the large basket opposite, the same color is picked up with Bidens ferulifolia, and the white-flowered petunias also help to emphasize the white window frame. The planting is so dense that the wooden cladding on the front of the house is completely obscured by the display.

The capillary matting is in direct contact with the soil. If it is damp, so is the soil.

1 *Feed the wick through the plastic base plate. It draws water up from the reservoir at the base of the basket and keeps the capillary matting damp.*

A self-watering spring basket

For people who are out of the house all day or who are a little forgetful when it comes to watering, a self-watering hanging basket is the perfect solution. Immediately after planting, water the basket in the normal way to ensure that the potting mixture is thoroughly wetted. Thereafter, water will be drawn up from the reservoir at the bottom of the basket, as and when the plants require it. If you use the tube to fill the reservoir, there is no danger of over-watering, as seep holes in the sides allow the excess to drain out.

In this display, a fresh scheme of yellow and white spring flowers and foliage contrasts with the dark green basket. As it has solid sides, all the planting has to go in the top of the basket, so pick at least one plant with long trails to soften the edge. This green-and-white variegated ivy with its finely pointed leaves stands out beautifully. White drumstick primulas pick up on the white-edged ivy and make a striking and unusual centerpiece. Their display is relatively long-lived, the spherical heads opening and developing over a number of weeks. When flowering has finished, transfer the plants to the garden, if possible to a spot with moisture-retentive soil and light shade. The glossy-leaved *Euonymus japonicus* 'Aureus' comes from the houseplant section of a garden center as pots of rooted cuttings. When this basket is dismantled, it should be possible to separate these out and pot them up individually.

2 *Push the watering tube through the hole in the base plate before adding potting mix and plants. You should be able to camouflage it easily.*

3 *Add a layer of moist potting mix, completely covering the capillary matting. Try the largest plant for size and adjust the level as necessary.*

4 *If the rootball is too big to fit in the basket, knock off any loose soil first and gently tease the roots apart at the base, so that they spread out flat.*

Use a peat-based potting mixture formulated for hanging baskets.

Primula denticulata 'Alba'
(white-flowered
drumstick primula)

Primula (hardy
hybrid primrose)

8 Hang the basket in a lightly shaded, sheltered spot. Continue watering via the tube. Remove individual blooms as they fade and cut off drumsticks when the whole head has finished flowering.

5 Add another primula and then fill in the gaps left on one side with the variegated euonymus. Put in more potting mix as you go.

Hedera helix
cultivar
(variegated ivy)

Euonymus
japonicus 'Aureus'

7 Split apart a couple of pots of rooted ivy cuttings and fit them around the edge of the basket. Fill any gaps with soil. Water the potting mix thoroughly in the usual way.

6 Plant two hardy primroses, one on either side of the watering tube. Leave space around the rim for some trailing plants. As well as ivy, try variegated periwinkle, aubretia or silver lamium.

Hyacinths and primulas

This scheme is a rich blend of jewel-colored primulas, red hyacinths and warm terracotta, shades more often associated with late summer. The new *Primula* 'Wanda' hybrids have introduced a whole set of colors for the spring garden - glowing purples, reds and blues, often further enhanced by dark foliage. Mixed trays of plants may contain white-, yellow- and pink-flowered forms, so if you want to copy this scheme, wait until one or two buds have opened to check the color or buy plants separately in flower. Heavily scented hyacinths can often be bought in bud as single bulbs and add a luxurious touch to plantings of this kind. Like the hybrid primroses, hyacinths now come in many different colors, including orange and creamy yellow, though as potted bulbs, pinks, blues and white still predominate.

The advantage of buying plants in single colors is that color scheming in mixed arrangements is so much easier. There are several, equally effective ways to approach color scheming; one is to stick to just one color of flower, but to vary the form and texture of the plants as much as possible, say an all-white or all-yellow scheme. Another is to pick two strongly contrasting colors, such as orange and blue, purple and yellow or cerise-pink and lime-green. The color scheme chosen for this wall pot illustrates another option, namely a blend of related colors and shades. The reverse 'cool' option to the one illustrated would be blues, purples, silver-white and lime-green.

4 *Place the hyacinths against the back wall of the basket, leaving space for the primulas in the foreground. You may need to shake some of the potting mixture from around the roots to create more room.*

Be sure to moisten the potting mix before use.

1 *Line a terracotta wall basket with black plastic to prevent evaporation through the sides. Cut a hole in the base in line with the drainage hole.*

2 *Put a flat stone over the hole to prevent soil loss and then add a shallow layer of gravel to provide good drainage for the plants.*

3 *Cover the gravel with potting mix. Always use fresh potting mix and never garden compost or soil, which contains too many pests and diseases.*

5 *Do not worry if the hyacinths look a little awkward at first; the primroses will soon cover up the base of the bulbs. Lay the plants out first, so that you can work out which are the best color combinations.*

6 *Squeeze the rootballs into an oval shape so that you can fit in as many plants as possible. Winter and spring baskets tend not to grow like summer ones, so cram them full for maximum impact.*

Some more schemes for spring

Silver Cineraria, *pale blue pansies and white polyanthus.*

Velvet-red pansies with Heuchera 'Palace Purple' *as the centerpiece; dark green ivy trails.*

White heather with Lamium 'White Nancy'.

Festuca glauca *as the centerpiece with red* Bellis *(double daisies).*

Slate-blue polyanthus, cream Viola *and* Euonymus japonicus 'Aureus'.

Pansy 'Imperial Antique Shades' F1 with blue-gray dwarf conifer.

Reddish pink hyacinths

Primula 'Wanda' hybrid

Terracotta wall basket with classical-style relief.

7 *The primroses will flower for several weeks if they are regularly watered and dead-headed. Hyacinths, however, are not as long-lived. Once their flowers have faded, cut off the heads, but keep the leaves intact.*

25

Buckets full of bulbs

Shiny metal pails make fun containers, especially for children's gardens, and are easily converted to hanging baskets with a length of silver-colored chain. This mixed planting of bulbs is unusual but works well because of the contrast of form and color. You can now buy a wide variety of potted bulbs, in bud or flower, between late winter and early spring. Dwarf varieties are particularly suited to hanging baskets, especially dwarf, multiheaded daffodils, grape hyacinths, chionodoxas, scillas and *Anemone blanda*, all of which flower over a relatively long period. Once flowering has finished, take the buckets off display, remove the faded heads and continue to feed and water, maintaining the foliage to allow the bulbs to build up reserves for flowering the following spring. As an alternative to bulbs, you could plant a whole collection of silver buckets with individual polyanthus or hardy primrose hybrids. Pick bright paintbox colors - red, yellow, blue and cerise for a cheerful welcome for visitors at the front of the house.

1 Put a layer of gravel or small pieces of broken styrofoam trays in the bucket to provide a drainage layer in these sealed containers.

Dividing clumps of bulbs

Provided you do not damage too many of the roots, you can separate out individual bulbs from their clumps quite safely. Water thoroughly a few hours beforehand to help them cope better with the stress.

Right: *Tease off as much soil as you can from the daffodil rootball, reducing its size to fit the bucket.*

Below: *Gently pull apart the rootball, separating individual bulbs for planting in narrow gaps.*

2 Add a little soil - use a gritty, free-draining mix if you do not intend to perforate the bucket base. Remove handles for easy planting.

Narcissus
'Tête à Tête'

6 Hang the buckets at head
height to appreciate the flowers
at close quarters. If using multiheaded daffodils, such as 'Tête à
Tête', pick off individual
flowers as they fade.

Chionodoxa luciliae

Muscari
armeniacum
(Grape hyacinth)

3 Remove some soil from around
the roots of the clump of daffodils.
Plant the bulbs, leaving enough space
around the edges for the muscari.

4 Using small,
teased-out
clumps or individual
grape hyacinth
bulbs, fill in round
the edge of the
daffodil centerpiece.
Squeeze in as many
bulbs as you can.
The flower heads
may droop a bit at
first but should re-
orientate themselves
after a few days.

5 This time, using
muscari for the
central planting,
make an outer ring
of the smaller, pale
blue-and-white
striped chionodoxas.
Cover any exposed
roots or bulbs with
more potting mix
and water carefully
to settle the soil.
Take care not to
overwater.

1 *Line the back and base of the basket with black plastic, tucking the top edge in behind the frame at the back to stop it slipping down later on.*

A spring wall basket

A large, manger-style basket can create an impressive wall feature to brighten up a bare expanse of brickwork. It could also be used like a windowbox, fixed beneath the frame. Though not very wide, there is room along the length for a good assortment of plants and because there are gaps between the bars, you can plant through the front easily. Putting pink and yellow plants next to each other in the garden is normally frowned upon, but this scheme just goes to show how rules about color combinations can often be broken with great success! Using the same types of plant, there are several other colorways that work well. For example, if you want a more vivid scheme, try scarlet red tulips, such as the dwarf 'Red Riding Hood', white daisies, deep blue polyanthus and blue-and-white violas. More ideas are suggested in the panel.

The polyanthus used in this scheme are the exact color of wild primroses and to take the wild theme a step further, the spaces between all the plants were filled with moss, giving the impression of a bank in the hedgerow filled with spring flowers. With the exception of the tulips, the flowers in this basket will keep blooming for weeks, provided they have been looked after properly. If the leaves begin to yellow and show signs of starvation, water with a liquid feed. Deadhead regularly and keep a watch for aphids and other pests, which can proliferate without warning during warm spells.

2 *Lift up the lining and tuck some moss underneath to hide the plastic. Add a thick layer of moss until it is high enough to add the first plants.*

3 *Break up bedding strips of violas and feed them through the bars at different heights for a more natural effect. Fill the gaps in between with potting mix.*

4 *Put three pots of tulips along the back, carefully breaking the roots apart so that the bulbs can be planted in more of a straight line, allowing room for the other flowers in the foreground.*

Schemes for spring

Yellow dwarf daffodils, blue Scilla siberica or Muscari (grape hyacinth) and red primroses planted with gold variegated ivy or variegated Vinca minor.

Dark purple tulips, light purple and mauve-pink shades of dwarf wallflowers and silver cineraria planted with green-leaved Lamium maculatum.

Scarlet-red, double-flowered Ranunculus, maroon-red Heuchera 'Palace Purple' and deep red Dicentra 'Bacchanal' planted with dark green ivy.

White heathers, white polyanthus, white pansy, white Lamium 'White Nancy'.

Skimmia japonica 'Rubella', Euonymus 'Emerald Gaiety' and Vinca minor trails.

5 *Add the yellow polyanthus in a zigzag line, leaving gaps in between for the double daisies. You may need to squeeze the rootballs out of shape to fit them in.*

Tulipa kaufmanniana 'The First'

Polyanthus 'Crescendo Primrose'

6 *Fill in any spaces with double daisies. Add potting mix around the plants and firm in gently. Cover any gaps with sphagnum moss and water the arrangement thoroughly.*

Bellis perennis (*double daisy*)

7 *Once the tulips have started to fade, carefully lift them out intact and plant them in the garden, where they can continue to grow and build up reserves for the following year. Replace them with more pot-grown bulbs and some spring-flowering herbaceous plants.*

Viola

Silver baskets of campanulas

Planted up, a pair of these tiny woven silver baskets would make a lovely gift. For a more natural look, there are plenty of tiny wicker baskets available, but whatever you choose, both the planting and method of hanging need to be on the same Lilliputian scale. One basket on its own is unlikely to make sufficient impact, so try two or more baskets hung at different heights, say from a curtain pole across a small window. In spring, you will often find outdoor plants mixed in with the houseplants in garden centers. These are forced into flower early to be used for temporary indoor decoration and may be planted outside once the display has finished. Campanulas and a variety of bulbs make popular subjects for forcing. Here, the lilac-blue blooms of an alpine bellflower (*Campanula* sp.) combine beautifully with the silver of the basket. The flowers and leaves are naturally small-scale, but growers can now produce temporarily miniaturized plants that flower at only a few inches tall. If you like the idea of using dwarf bulbs in baskets, try potting some up in the fall and grow them on through the winter in a cold frame. Once you can see color in the flower buds, plant them in the baskets and bring them indoors. Try chionodoxa, scilla, crocus and puschkinia.

1 Have the baskets to hand when choosing your plants and other materials, such as the ribbon, to see if the combinations will work well.

2 To prevent drips, line the basket with a square of transparent plastic. Fold the corners to fit and trim off any excess at the top with scissors.

3 Add some gravel or charcoal chippings to provide drainage, but take care not to overwater, especially when using drought-tolerant plants.

Campanula *sp.*
(alpine bellflower)

4 Try the campanulas in the baskets to work out the best arrangement. There may not be room for any potting mix in the base.

5 Now plant the campanulas; allow some foliage to trail over the basket sides. Fill the gaps between plants with potting mix so that there are no air spaces. Add sufficient water to settle the soil.

6 Hang the baskets in a cool, well-lit position. Suspend them using fine florist's ribbon. If the baskets are a gift, you could add some extra ribbon loops and corkscrew curls to the handle as well.

Mini basket plants

Cyclamen persicum *(mini cyclamen)*
Dendranthema *(mini pot mum)*
Exacum affine *(mini Persian violet)*
Kalanchoe blossfeldiana *(mini flaming Katy)*, Rosa *(mini rose)*
Saintpaulia ionantha *(mini African violet)*
Houseplant 'tots' from garden centers make good, temporarily small, foliage plants for very small containers.

A cottage garden basket

This wicker basket has a rustic look, so the planting style is soft and relaxed, just like a traditional cottage garden border. *Campanula carpatica* 'Blue Clips', a hardy alpine bellflower that is sometimes brought into flower early and sold as a temporary indoor plant, is teamed with a gold-leaved trailing ivy. Plenty of other hardy herbaceous plants and tender perennials would produce a similar effect, including the dwarf marguerites (*Argyranthemum frutescens* cultivars, such as 'Petite Pink'), and dwarf scabious, *Scabiosa* 'Butterfly Blue' and 'Pink Mist', which flower over a long period. A semi-trailing fuchsia, such as the frilly-petalled 'Swingtime', would work well in combination with the trailing *Verbena* 'Sissinghurst' or paler pink 'Silver Anne', both vigorous and with a strong mildew resistance. Many hardy annuals, grown in pots and transferred to the basket when large enough, would also give the required 'cottage' look. Try *Nasturtium* 'Alaska', with its white-marbled leaves, the pot marigold mix *Calendula* 'Fiesta Gitana' or *Brachycome iberidifolia* 'Summer Skies', which produces a profusion of blue, purple and white daisies all summer. Several pansies are now available in appropriately old-fashioned pastel shades. Try *Viola* 'Watercolours' or 'Romeo and Juliet'.

4 *Arrange the longest trails of ivy to create a rim of greenery that spills out over the basket's dipped edge. Make the composition asymmetric.*

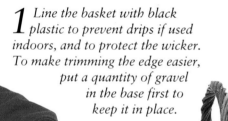

1 *Line the basket with black plastic to prevent drips if used indoors, and to protect the wicker. To make trimming the edge easier, put a quantity of gravel in the base first to keep it in place.*

2 *Add more gravel or bits of broken styrofoam plant trays to create a drainage reservoir to prevent overwatering.*

3 *For seasonal arrangements indoors and out, use a peat-based potting mix. For border perennials and alpines, use a soil-based mixture or add coarse grit to the potting mix.*

With a wide handle like this, use a butcher's hook to suspend the basket from the chain.

7 Water the basket and hang it in a cool, well-lit spot indoors, such as a conservatory or large glass porch. Pick off dead blooms regularly, and after flowering, harden off the campanulas and plant them in the garden.

Campanula carpatica 'Blue Clips'

This Hedera helix *cultivar (a variegated ivy) combines well with the blue of the bellflower and stands out against the dark-colored wicker.*

5 Fill the center of the basket with the campanulas. Try not to hide the handle, as this is very much part of the overall design. Fill any gaps with soil and firm in lightly.

6 Break off chunks of rooted ivy cuttings and use these to fill in any gaps that remain around the edge of the basket.

33

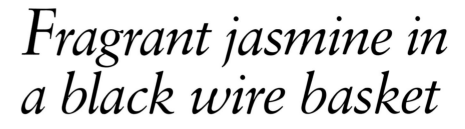

Fragrant jasmine in a black wire basket

There need only be a few flowers open for you to detect the presence of jasmine. The perfume is intoxicating and a single plant in full flower can fill a large room with fragrance. Jasmine makes a wonderful basket plant because of its graceful trailing habit and delicate foliage and flower clusters, but it is vigorous and will ultimately need replanting into a large pot or conservatory border.

In garden centers, you will often see indoor climbers and lax shrubs trained round hoops. This is just a way of presenting the plant tidily and is not necessary for its cultivation. Following on from the spring-flowering jasmine, you will find summer-flowering climbers, such as the passion flower *(Passiflora caerulea)*, Cape leadwort *(Plumbago auriculata)*, *Abutilon* hybrids and black-eyed Susan *(Thunbergia alata)*. All of these can be replanted to become unusual and eye-catching subjects for hanging baskets. The delicate black-eyed Susan combines well with other plants (see page 72), but the others are best planted singly in large baskets, and, like the jasmine, transferred to more conventional containers at the end of the season. The wirework basket for this project was chosen for its elegant lines and emphasizes the romantic feel created by the jasmine's airy trails.

1 Gently pull out the wire hoop and begin to untangle the stems. This can be a slow and fiddly process, but should not be hurried.

2 Although you could line this basket with plastic, you can achieve the most attractive effect with moist sphagnum moss. Mist spray the moss regularly to keep it fresh.

3 Pack the moss lining in tightly to make a thick dense layer that prevents the potting mix drying out too quickly or washing out through gaps when the basket is watered.

4 *Add a little potting mixture to the fully lined basket. A special hanging basket mix would be ideal, as water will tend to be lost more rapidly than normal through the basket sides. Plant, filling in the gaps with more potting mix.*

Jasminum polyanthum

5 *Spread out the trailing jasmine stems so that they hang evenly over the sides of the basket. Then take one or two of the longest trails and wind them carefully round to cover the handle of the basket.*

6 *To persuade the stems to trail down in the desired position, fix them in place using long 'pins' made from bent florist's wire. Push the pins through the sphagnum moss.*

7 *Hang the finished basket in a well-lit position. Remove individual flowers as they fade, using a sharp pair of nail scissors. Water by plunging the basket in a bucket or bowl of tepid water. This will also rewet the moss.*

35

Painting pots for a weathered look

Nowadays, you can obtain a wide range of plastic terracotta-effect pots. These have the advantage of being unbreakable, frost-proof and lightweight. Some are more realistic than others, but all have a rather raw, brand new look about them. Over a period of time, real terracotta weathers and takes on the patina of age. White salt deposits work through to the surface and in damp, shady conditions, a coating of green algae often appears. Using a variety of simple paint techniques, it is possible to mimic this transformation and achieve a realistic effect on plastic containers. Pots and planters with a high relief are the most convincing when painted, as the dark and light shading emphasizes the contours. Acrylic paint, mixed and thinned with water, is an ideal medium for this technique as it remains wet and soluble for long enough to work on and correct any mistakes, but then dries to form an effective waterproof plastic coating.

1 *Mix up a small quantity of white, yellow and dark green artist's acrylic paints, adding water until the mixture becomes quite thin and runny. Tilt the wallbasket back slightly and apply the first coat.*

2 *Cover the face with a liberal quantity of paint. You need not be too particular at this stage and you will notice that the color tends to run off the raised portions and collect in the grooves.*

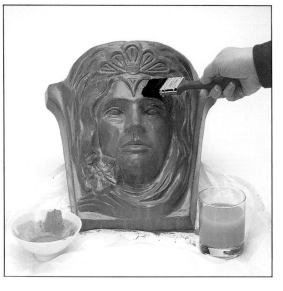

3 *If the color is too opaque and the terracotta does not start to show through after a couple of minutes, use a clean, wet brush and go over the raised portions of the face again, diluting the paint.*

4 *Use a piece of absorbent kitchen towel, scrunched up into a pad and dampened slightly, to dab off some of the paint from raised parts of the face. Do this in irregular patches.*

Plecostachys serpyllifolia

Argyranthemum frutescens *(marguerite)*

5 Once dry, apply a second coat. Adjust the mix if the first coat was too dark or light. In this case, extra white and yellow were added.

6 The paint runs down in streaks, much like weathering caused by damp conditions. Pigments separate out, adding to the illusion of age.

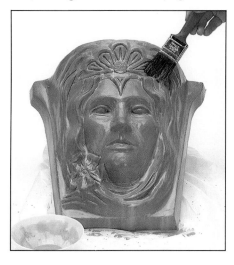

Create a sense of mystery in the garden by half hiding the face on a wall or fence covered in foliage. Trim plants to keep them in proportion with the head and remove dead blooms.

7 When dry, mix up some dark green paint and water. Using a damp, natural sponge, dab over the surface and work paint into the crevices of the face.

8 When dry, plant up the head with flowers and foliage to enhance the weathered face. Soft, old-fashioned and 'neutral' colors work well.

A character wall pot with ivy hair

A wall pot decorated with a carved face adds a theatrical touch to the garden. These ancient craggy features and untamed beard merely needed some wild locks to frame them and what better plant to choose than trailing ivy? Other 'hair' alternatives include the evergreen grasses and grasslike plants, such as *Carex* species and varieties - try 'Snowline' or 'Evergold' - and the blue-leaved fescues *(Festuca)*. Whatever you use, keep the planting of such pots as simple as possible to highlight rather than compete with the decoration. Double the dramatic effect by using two identical pots on either side of a doorway or, for a classical look, try mounting a single head at the top of a trellis 'pillar' to provide a focus for a bare piece of wall. Wall pots are often made from terracotta or cast cement, which looks like carved stone. They are usually quite small, with room for just a few plants and because they only hold a limited volume of soil, plants tend to dry out quickly. Pick the largest possible container and line unglazed terracotta with plastic to prevent excessive water loss through the sides. Choose plants that withstand occasional drying out - succulents and silver-leaved plants are ideal for pots attached to a hot, sunny wall.

2 Instead of drilling holes in the base of the container, fill the narrow space in the bottom section with gravel to provide drainage.

3 Cover the gravel with potting mixture, filling the wall pot but allowing space on top for the ivies. Try one of the plants for size.

'Meta'

'Adam'

'Golden Ester'

'Sagittifolia Variegata'

1 Ivy is mostly used as a foil for flowers, but this blend of plain and variegated Hedera helix *becomes a feature in its own right, creating the effect of silver-streaked hair.*

'Mini Heron'

'Goldchild'

Arrange ivy trails against the wall like wisps of unruly hair.

6 *Fill the gaps between the plants with more potting mixture, and water the plants. Hang the pot on two screws fixed into the wall. A sheltered, shady position is ideal to prevent damage by cold winds or scorching in strong summer sunlight.*

This plastic pot has been painted to look like weathered terracotta (see page 36).

4 *Squeeze the rootballs into ovals so that you can plant as many different kinds of ivy in the top as possible to make a thick head of hair.*

5 *Remember that the basket will be hung against a wall, so arrange some plants so that they stick up at the back.*

1 *Assemble a mixture of flowering and foliage plants, with trailing and creeping varieties to cover the basket sides and bushy, upright types for the middle.*

Planting up for summer

The sooner you can plant up your summer baskets, the sooner they will start flowering. Baskets kept under glass until they are well established not only look better when hung outdoors, but also tend to be more resilient in unfavorable conditions. So, if you have a conservatory or frost-free greenhouse, you could start planting in early spring. Remember, however, that in cold areas prone to late frosts, you may have to keep baskets under cover until early summer. There is no shortage of basket plants at the very start of the season. Garden centers now sell a wide range of seedlings and rooted cuttings in small pots or 'plugs'. Some of these are perforated, allowing the roots to grow through the sides and are designed to be planted pot-and-all to lessen the shock of transplanting. These young plants are commonly referred to as 'tots'. They make planting up the sides of baskets a relatively simple affair and, unlike 'strip' bedding, plants suffer little or no root damage.

Net pots can be left in place during planting, but you must remove solid pots.

5 *Gently push the rooted cuttings through the basket sides. The neck of the plant should be just inside the wire and packed with sphagnum moss to prevent moisture loss. Cover the root-ball with more mix, filling in any gaps.*

2 *Cut out a circle of black plastic and place it in the bottom of the basket. This acts as a water reservoir and helps prevent soil loss. Add some potting mixture to hold it in place.*

3 *Tuck a layer of sphagnum moss under the edge of the plastic to disguise it. Once the basket is full, you will not notice the plastic at all.*

4 *Build up the sides with a thick layer of moist sphagnum moss. Pack it in tightly to prevent soil escaping when the plants are watered. Add more mix. Continue until you reach the level intended for the first row of plants.*

6 Plant the large ivy, by holding the rootball horizontally and feeding the long trails through the basket sides from the inside out. Push the crown of the plant hard against the inside of the basket.

7 When the basket sides are planted up, add sufficient potting mix to cover all the exposed rootballs. Leave enough space for planting in the top.

8 Add more trailing plants to hang over the top edge of the basket. Fill in the center with upright plants, leaving room for proper development.

9 Cover the surface with a thick layer of moss. Water the basket well and hang it in a light, frost-free place until the plants are established.

10 Once young plants develop a good root system, they quickly fill out the basket. Feed them regularly to keep them flowering.

Fuchsia 'Beacon' (bush variety)

Fuchsia 'La Campanella' (cascade variety)

Verbena 'Blue Cascade'

Hedera helix (variegated ivy)

Glechoma hederacea 'Variegata'

Brachycome multifida

A shallow basket

Trugs are traditionally used for collecting cut flowers, fruit and vegetables from the garden. The attractive one in this scheme is made of thin strips of curved wood held together by a bamboo frame that adds an oriental touch. The clear, rich colors of the planting scheme complement the neutral shade of the trug, with lacquer-red picking up on the oriental theme.

New Guinea hybrid *Impatiens* are like giant-flowered versions of the ordinary busy Lizzie. The flower colors are vibrant and the long, tapering leaves are either green, bronze or brightly variegated. There are many types to choose from and all make superb, long-lasting additions to indoor displays. To keep plants compact and bushy, they need a little more light than bedding *Impatiens*, but keep them out of direct sunlight. They can be grown outdoors in summer, but perform best in a relatively warm, sheltered and humid environment, such as a lightly shaded conservatory or greenhouse. The creeping fig *(Ficus pumila)* thrives in similar conditions and its small, heart-shaped leaves and wiry, trailing habit make it a good partner for the bold *Impatiens*. The tropical red flowers seem to glow all the more strongly surrounded by pure greenery. There is a creeping fig with white-variegated foliage, but the leaves are very bright and would compete for attention in a scheme such as this.

1 As this is a ready-lined container, you will need to add some gravel to provide drainage. Expanded clay pellets for use in gravel trays are also suitable.

3 Place the first of the two Impatiens in the basket, turning it so that the stems fit round the handle. If the basket is to be viewed from one side only, you can tilt the plant to give a fuller effect.

2 Add a layer of potting mixture. Make sure that the plants have been given a thorough soaking beforehand. Try the largest plant in the trug for size to gauge the depth of soil required.

Use peat-based multipurpose or houseplant potting mixture.

New Guinea hybrid
Impatiens.

7 Hang up the basket using natural colored rope or twine. Mist spray daily and do not allow the potting mixture to dry out between waterings.

4 Fill the middle of the basket with the other Impatiens. Planting off-center with some overhanging stems looks more natural.

5 Lift the foliage so that you can fit the creeping figs underneath. Fill the gaps around the rootballs with potting mix as you work.

Ficus pumila
(creeping fig)

6 Squeeze in as many of these 'filler' plants as you can to create a really lush effect. Arrange them so that the trailing foliage looks as though it is growing out between the Impatiens.

Above: Wirework baskets tend to be costly; whereas ordinarily you would not mind if a basket became smothered by exuberant growth, here you will want to display at least some of the intricate decoration.

Red geraniums in an elegant wirework basket

Romantic, Edwardian-style wirework is back in fashion and you can now buy quite a wide range of elegant designs. The plants in this scheme were chosen to match the delicate framework. Zonal geraniums *(Pelargonium)* would have been too heavy-looking, with their solid flower heads and large rounded leaves. Ivy-leaved geraniums are far better suited; their wiry stems, covered in attractive foliage, create a much more open and airy effect. Since most baskets are viewed from below, some foliage or flower detail in the sides of the basket is essential. The brightly variegated kingfisher daisy is a good choice here, as it enjoys the same conditions as the geraniums and never gets too vigorous. Sky blue daisies sometimes appear later in the season and these would complement the rich crimson-red geranium flowers. Other suitable plants for this style of basket include tender perennials, such as the lilac blue-flowered *Brachycome multifida,* with its feathery foliage and a profusion of daisy flowers, *Argyranthemum* 'Petite Pink', a delicate dwarf marguerite with shell-pink blooms, and single fuchsias, like the red-flowered cascade variety 'Marinka'.

1 Line the back and base of the basket with plastic to prevent damp seeping into the wall behind. Trim off any excess at the top or tuck it behind the frame.

2 Using thick clumps of moist sphagnum moss, begin lining the front of the basket. Tuck some between the wire and the plastic for camouflage.

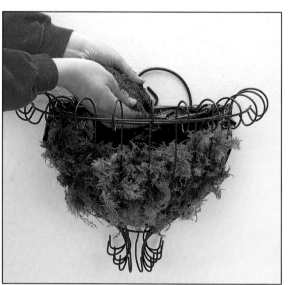

3 Firm down the moss so that it forms a solid barrier. Add potting mixture up to the point where you intend to plant through the front of the basket.

4 Guide the shoots of the kingfisher daisies between the wires. Rest the rootball horizontally on the soil. Vary planting heights to avoid straight lines.

5 Fill around the plants with more moss, making sure that the neck of the plant is far enough inside the basket to avoid the risk of drying out.

6 Now add the first of the ivy-leaved trailing geraniums, arranging the trailing stems so that they point out to the side.

Ivy-leaved geranium 'Barock'

Deadhead flowers as soon as they start to fade.

7 Finish planting the top of the basket, making a balanced arrangement that is wider at the top than at the base.

8 Fill in any gaps with soil, and water the arrangement thoroughly. Hang it up by hooking the frame over two screws fixed into a sunny wall.

Variegated Felicia amelloides

45

1 *Cut a piece of plastic from an old potting mixture bag and place it black-side-down in the bottom of the basket, to act as a water reservoir.*

2 *Fill the plastic 'dish' with moist, soilless potting mix. Even when the top of the basket is dry, the plant roots should find moisture here.*

3 *Using thick clumps of moist sphagnum moss, line the basket sides. Tuck moss under the edges of the plastic as camouflage.*

4 *Build up the front with bedding violas pushed horizontally through the bars. Pack in as many as will fit to create a really full display.*

A summer basket with a purple theme

This basket contains an unusual mixture of plants in subtle shades of purple and silver-gray. The deep velvet-purple bedding viola 'Prince Henry' makes a superb contrast with the other flowers and foliage and is just right for covering the basket sides. In the top are the daisylike flowers of *Osteospermum* 'Sunny Lady', the deepest color in the 'Sunny' series. Like all osteospermums, the flowers close in shade, so hang the basket where it will receive sun for most of the day. *Nemesia fruticans* is relatively new and, perhaps surprisingly, is being marketed as a basket and container plant. The more familiar *Nemesia* is known to be intolerant of drought, but its relative certainly seems to be much more resilient, producing airy flowers all summer long. The foliage in this basket ranges from the fine, feathery leaves of *Lotus berthelotii* to the cut leaves of cineraria and the rounded, leathery, purple foliage of *Sedum* 'Bertram Anderson'. You will find this plant in the herbaceous perennial section of the garden center or nursery.

5 *Use more sphagnum moss to fill the gaps between the plants, so that the rootballs are protected from drying out and to prevent soil escaping when you water the basket.*

6 *Next add a group of cineraria, tilting one down over the basket sides to soften the edge. Pinch out the tips of these plants to keep them compact and bushy in shape.*

7 Plant the large sedum to one side so that its long trailing shoots hang over the edge. In mid- to late summer it produces crimson-red flowers.

8 Plant nemesias to give height at the back. The lotus at the front trails over the edge; remove any orange-red flowers that appear later on.

Osteospermum 'Sunny Lady'

Nemesia fruticans. *Cut back faded flower stems to promote further blooms.*

Sedum 'Bertram Anderson'

Viola 'Prince Henry'

Senecio cineraria

Lotus berthelotii (coral gem)

9 Fill in the remaining space at the back with the osteospermum and cover all the exposed rootballs with potting mixture. Water thoroughly and add more soil if gaps appear.

10 To aid moisture retention, add a thick layer of moist sphagnum moss over the potting mix in the top of the basket. Allow plants to settle in for several days by standing the basket in a sheltered shady spot.

Hostas in a woodland basket for a shady place

With the exception of the variegated ivy, all the plants in this basket come from the herbaceous perennials section of the garden center. There is no reason why plants from any category - alpine, shrub, herbaceous or houseplant - cannot be used temporarily in a hanging basket, providing they are the right size with an attractive habit and long-lasting color. More drought-tolerant types are obviously better suited, as it is very difficult to keep any basket constantly moist. A number of flowering bedding plants thrive in shade, including *Fuchsia, Impatiens, Lobelia* and *Begonia*. Team them with ivies or gold-leaved foliage plants, such as the feathery golden feverfew (*Tanacetum parthenium* 'Aureum'), golden creeping Jenny *(Lysimachia nummularia* 'Aurea') or a gold-leaved hosta. Silver and gray-leaved plants do not normally tolerate shade, which is why the silver-leaved lamiums, including 'White Nancy' and 'Pink Pewter', make such useful basket plants. Some of the fernlike dicentras more often associated with woodland gardening also work well in shade. Here, 'Pearl Drops' makes a wonderful contrast with the golden hosta.

4 *Add the gold-leaved hosta 'August Moon'. As well as strikingly architectural foliage, it produces pale pink bellflower spikes in midsummer.*

1 *There are various options for lining hanging baskets, many of which use recycled or waste materials, such as this coir matting, a by-product of the coconut industry. Wool, foam and paper are also used.*

Stand the basket in the top of a large flower pot to keep it stable while you work.

2 *Pour in some moisture-retentive potting mix - one designed for baskets is ideal. Here, the thick liner also protects plants from drying out.*

3 *Plant the dicentra, as with all plants, leaving enough of a gap at the top to allow for watering. 'Pearl Drops' goes on flowering all summer.*

Hosta 'August Moon'

Dicentra 'Pearl Drops' has blue-gray foliage.

5 *Plant ground-covering lamium in the rest of the basket. This variety produces a profusion of pink-hooded flowers in early and midsummer.*

6 *The lamium will grow out, but for instant trails, add rooted cuttings of a gold-variegated* Hedera helix *variety.*

7 *When the basket is full of plants, fill in any gaps with potting mix. Add a thick layer of moist sphagnum moss or fine chipped bark as a water-retaining mulch.*

Hedera helix *cultivar (ivy)*

Lamium maculatum 'Pink Pewter', a pale rose-flowered variety.

8 *Hang the basket in a sheltered shaded site. At the end of the season, transfer the plants to the garden or plant them together in a wooden half barrel with some dwarf spring bulbs for a woodland effect.*

49

A pink basket for cool shade

Busy Lizzies *(Impatiens)* are invaluable for baskets as they come in such a wide range of colors, from almost fluorescent reds, pinks and purples to soft pastel shades and white. There are varieties with white-striped petals, pale varieties with darker 'eyes' or picotee types, such as the one illustrated, with darker-edged petals. Single F1 hybrid bedding varieties tend to give the best performance outdoors. You can get pretty doubles, too, but these tend to be less resistant to poor weather conditions. Busy Lizzies thrive in shade but will also grow happily in full sun, although some darker-flowered varieties can bleach unless given some shelter at midday. Here, a soft pink shade has been selected to highlight the pink-splashed leaves of the variegated tradescantia. Try teaming up white-variegated apple mint or spider plants *(Chlorophytum)* with pure white impatiens or, for a more vibrant alternative, match orange, cerise-pink or red impatiens with the variegation on *Solenostemon* (coleus) leaves.

The trailing forms of tradescantia, including white-, pink- and purple-variegated, as well as plain-leaved, are popular houseplants and easy to propagate. Outdoors, grow them in sun or moderate shade, but avoid deep shade as variegated forms may revert to all-green. If you start propagating in early spring, you can have plenty of strong young plants ready for hardening off and planting in early summer. Alternatively, buy houseplant 'tots' and pot them on to promote rapid growth prior to planting. Several other houseplants perform well outdoors in summer (see panel).

3 Plant the basket sides using bedding impatiens with a relatively small rootball, such as those sold in divided trays as opposed to pots. Push the rootball through the gaps and rest it horizontally on the soil inside.

1 Line the back and base of the basket with black plastic to protect the wall and prevent soil loss when watering. Camouflage with a thick layer of sphagnum moss.

2 Continue to line the front of the basket with moss, leaving a gap near the top to allow for planting. Fill the base with a mixture recommended for hanging baskets.

4 Surround the neck of the plants with more moss to prevent soil leakage and to help prevent the roots from drying out. Add more impatiens in the top of the basket to soften the edges.

6 Add more tradescantias until the basket is full. Alternatively, leave a gap at the back and plant extra impatiens that will grow taller and give the display a more circular outline.

5 Plant a variegated tradescantia in the top and arrange the trails so that they cover the bare moss at the front. Pinch out the shoot tips occasionally to keep plants well clothed in leaves.

Tradescantia fluminensis 'Tricolor'. Choose a bushy, compact specimen. Remove any all-green shoots that appear.

Houseplants outside

Abutilon megapotamicum 'Variegatum', Asparagus densiflorus *Sprengeri Group*, Asparagus setaceus *(syn.* A. plumosus), Begonia sutherlandii, Ceropegia woodii, Chlorophytum comosum 'Variegatum', Kalanchoe blossfeldiana, Saxifraga stolonifera, Scirpus cernuus, Soleirolia soleirolii *(formerly* Helxine), Solenostemon (Coleus), Tolmiea menziesii 'Taff's Gold', Tradescantia zebrina

Impatiens 'Super Elfin Swirl' F1

7 Fill in any gaps with soil and water well. Hang on a shady, sheltered wall, using two screws fixed with wall plugs.

Thyme, sage and verbena

Variegated and colored-leaved herbs make attractive additions to baskets and wall planters. They often perform better than more conventional basket plants in hot, dry summers, thriving in the well-drained conditions and not minding the occasional missed watering. They also smell good, so hang them where people can gently rub the foliage and release the aromatic oils. In general, variegated herbs are not as strongly flavored as plain-leaved species, but their foliage is useful for garnishing dishes and drinks. If you are growing herbs in a basket for the kitchen, you could plant a combination of good culinary types along with more decorative varieties and add a few edible flowers, such as nasturtium, *Calendula* (pot marigold) and viola for extra color. Herbs add significantly to the range of foliage plants that you can use in baskets. For baskets in full sun, try sages, such as the all-purple *Salvia officinalis* 'Purpurascens', the pretty pink, white and purple variegated *S. o.* 'Tricolor' or the yellow-variegated *S. o.* 'Icterina'. Creeping thymes are useful all year round for covering the sides of baskets - plant bushier, more upright types in the top. There are many golden and variegated varieties to choose from and you will find them in both the herb and alpine sections of garden centers. For baskets in shade, try using one of the variegated mints, golden marjoram or the feathery leaved golden feverfew.

4 *Plant the gold-variegated lemon thyme in the center of the wall pot to soften the edge. Add a variegated sage behind and slightly to one side. The sage will need pinching out to keep it bushy and in scale with the container.*

1 *Terracotta wall pots in sunny positions lose moisture rapidly, so always line them with plastic before planting. Cut a hole in it for drainage.*

2 *To ensure that the hole at the bottom does not clog up with potting mixture, add a layer of gravel or stone chippings before filling the planter with soil.*

3 *For a seasonal mixture of herbs and bedding plants, use a peat-based multi-purpose potting mix. For longer-term herb plantings, choose a soil-based mix.*

5 Plant a white-flowered trailing or upright verbena in the center and another variegated sage to match the one on the opposite side. Deep cerise-pink, scarlet, purple or golden-yellow flowers would work equally well.

6 Fill in the gaps at each end with more verbenas. Most trailing types will need cutting back now and then to keep them under control. This may not be necessary with the blue-purple cascade variety, which has more delicate foliage and flower.

Salvia officinalis *'Icterina'*

Verbena *'Sissinghurst White'*

7 Hang the arrangement on a wall that is in sun for at least half the day. Feed and water regularly. Keep a watch for powdery mildew on the verbenas and spray them with a systemic fungicide at the first sign.

Thymus *x* citriodorus *'Aureus'*

A spring basket

At the end of summer, dismantle the basket, removing the salvias and verbenas. You could leave the thyme in position and fill the space behind with crocus bulbs, such as Crocus chrysanthus 'Cream Beauty' or 'Zwanenburg Bronze', or gentian blue Scilla sibirica. Pack the bulbs in tightly for a good display in early spring. Or remove all the plants and replace them with blue or purple winter-flowering pansies.

1 *Line the back and base of the basket with black plastic. Line the front of the basket with sphagnum moss, tucking it under the plastic.*

2 *Pour some potting mix into the base of the basket. Put in the first row of widely spaced* Ageratum. *Rest the rootballs horizontally on the soil.*

A *summer display in a manger basket*

This scheme shows how easy it is to give the same container a whole new look, simply by choosing very different plants to fill it (see page 28 for alternative spring displays). Large containers such as these give far greater scope for combining plants creatively; generally speaking, the bigger the container, the more types of flower and foliage you can use to fill it, especially if you choose a fairly tight color scheme.

When selecting plants for a container, it pays to imagine what size and shape they will be after several weeks of growth. That way you will avoid the situation where one plant becomes out of proportion with the rest. This is not always easy, since information on the plant label can be rather sketchy and most young plants are of a similar size when you buy them. You will often need to trim back individual plants and it is better to begin to control vigorous types early on. For example, in the scheme featured here, you will need to pinch out the silver-leaved cinerarias occasionally to keep them bushy, as well as remove over-large leaves or shoots in the coming weeks.

3 *Build up the front with pink* Impatiens *and more* Ageratum, *varying the height of the plants so that the arrangement looks more natural.*

4 *To stabilize plants and prevent the rootballs from drying out, pack in plenty of moist sphagnum moss around their necks. Alternatively, line the whole of the front with plastic and cut holes in it for the plants.*

5 *Add more potting mix to cover the rootballs, making sure that it is well worked in between the plants to avoid leaving air pockets.*

6 Plant three zonal geraniums at the back. Look for plants labelled C.V.I. (Culture Virus Indexed), which have more flowers of a better size and color.

8 Add F1 hybrid petunias between the geraniums and cineraria. These floribunda types are compact, free-flowering and weather resistant.

9 Work potting mix into the gaps and cover with sphagnum moss. Water well. Hook the basket onto a sunny wall with two large protruding screws.

Petunia *(F1 hybrid 'Mirage Series')*

Pelargonium *(F1 hybrid PAC 'Fox')*

Senecio cineraria

7 Plant a row of cut-leaved cinerarias at the front for a splash of silver and to provide strong textural contrast. Tilt them forward to cover the basket edge.

Impatiens *(F1 hybrid 'Novette Series')*

Ageratum *(F1 hybrid 'Blue Danube')*

A classic white arrangement

1 Stand the basket on a bucket for stability. Cut a circle from an old potting mix bag and place it black side down in the base of the basket. Fill the plastic circle with potting mix.

If you seek to create a feeling of tranquillity and purity in your garden, consider how restful a combination of white, gray, silver and green foliage can be. However, for any monochrome scheme to be truly successful, it is important to have plenty of textural contrast between the different elements. In the basket featured here, the large, solid flower heads of petunia are planted alongside the smaller-flowered busy Lizzie and the busy Lizzie is in turn set against the froth of white alyssum. Foliage is no less important. The ferny, gray-leaved lotus has a totally different feel to the trailing ivy and both make a good contrast with the large, rounded leaves of the geranium. Bear in mind that there is a noticeable variation in the color of white flowers. Those in the basket are pure white and work well together, but the results would not have been so successful if it combined creamy whites and pure whites. Adding tiny amounts of an entirely different color will often lift an all-white scheme and make the flowers stand out all the more. Try adding the cream-variegated form of the blue, daisy-flowered *Felicia amelloides* to a creamy-white scheme or add warmth with the trailing geranium 'L'Elégante, whose variegated leaves and flowers are flushed pink. There are several other good white-variegated basket plants to choose from, including the aromatic and drought-resistant *Plectranthus coleoides* 'Marginatus', trailing nepeta or variegated ground ivy (*Glechoma hederacea* 'Variegata') and the variegated succulent trailer *Sedum lineare* 'Variegatum'. For gray and silver, choose from *Helichrysum petiolare*, *Senecio cineraria* and *Cerastium tomentosum*.

2 The plastic acts as a reservoir for the plants, trapping water and preventing soil from washing through. Tuck sphagnum moss under the edges for camouflage.

3 Cover the basket sides with the sweetly scented white alyssum, feeding the rootballs through the gaps to rest horizontally on the soil.

4 Pack moss around the necks of the plants to protect them from drying out. Angle the busy Lizzie so that it covers the rim of the basket.

Pelargonium PAC
cultivar 'Aphrodite'
(zonal geranium)

Impatiens
(busy Lizzie)

Petunia
'Celebrity White'

Lotus berthelotii
(coral gem)

5 *Plant a pot of the ferny* Lotus
berthelotii *to trail over the edge.
Next, begin planting petunias into
the top and sides of the basket.*

6 *Continue to build up the
basket sides with moss and
plants and work soil in around the
rootballs. Next add a trailing ivy.*

Lobularia
maritima 'Snow
Crystals' (sweet
white alyssum)

Hedera helix
(variegated ivy)

8 *Replace the chains and
hang the basket in a
sunny position where
passers-by can appreciate
the scent of the alyssum.*

7 *Squeeze a white-flowered
geranium into the space left in the
center of the basket. Fill any remaining
gaps with soil and water copiously.*

A romantic wall basket

Tissue paper begonias and airy asparagus fern give this wall basket the feel of a bouquet of flowers, and the rose-pink color scheme adds to the air of romance. This is a display for a site sheltered from wind and the bleaching effect of strong sunlight, where the luxuriant foliage and flowers can continue to grow unscathed. The large-leaved tuberous begonias are normally sold singly, in flower, making it easy to choose just the right shade. The F1 hybrid variety 'Non-Stop' is always a good choice and widely available, but it requires a little attention if it is to put on a really good show. The main task is to remove the two single female flowers with their winged seedpods that lie on either side of the central male flower. This will help the plant to produce much larger and more showy double flowers. Also remove dead flowers and leaves regularly to reduce the risk of botrytis (gray mold).

Since hanging baskets are nearly always attached to the walls of a house, it follows that planting schemes should blend with or emphasize the architecture around them. This basket would work well on an elegant period-style building, but might look out of place on the walls of an ultramodern town house. Choose a scheme that picks up colors used in and around the house and garden, say, the color of a front door, garden gate, shutters, wooden cladding or trellis. Orange-red brickwork can make a difficult backdrop for baskets, especially those with pink flowers. The 'safe' answer is to pick schemes containing 'neutral' silvers, grays and white, blues and purples, but baskets can be even more eye-catching featuring flame reds, oranges and touches of cream or planted with golden-yellow flowers and bronze-purple, blue-gray and silver foliage.

1 *Line the back of the basket with plastic cut from an old potting mix bag. Turn up a lip at the base to act as a water reservoir.*

2 *Line the front of the basket with a thick layer of moist sphagnum moss, packing it tightly to avoid losing potting mixture through the bars.*

3 *Turning the plant on its side, feed the stems of the lamium carefully through the bars so that it covers the front of the basket.*

4 *Add potting mix to support and cover the rootball, then continue to build up the moss lining across the front and sides of the basket.*

5 *Split up a tray of bedding begonias and feed plants through the bars to fill in around the lamium stems. The plants will soon spread to cover the moss.*

6 Add an asparagus fern. (Harden this off outdoors in advance.) Leave a gap at the front for more bedding begonias. Trim off any sections of leaf that bleach or lose their needles.

7 Fill in any spaces in the basket with more bedding begonias. Add the large-flowered begonias and then add sufficient soil and sphagnum moss to cover plant roots.

Asparagus setaceus *(Asparagus fern)* - not a fern at all but a relative of the lily.

Begonia x tuberhybrida *(tuberous-rooted begonia)*

Begonia *x* tuberhybrida

8 Water the basket well and do not allow it to dry out. The basket soon fills out; trim the lamium to keep it bushy. You can overwinter the fleshy begonia tubers in a frost-free place and bring the asparagus fern indoors as a houseplant.

Begonia semperflorens 'Olympia Pink' F1 *(fibrous-rooted, or bedding begonias)*

Lamium maculatum 'Pink Pearls' *(deadnettle) - a hardy herbaceous ground cover plant.*

A wall basket of portulacas for a hot sunny spot

Vibrantly colored portulacas are the perfect choice for this little Mexican-style wall pot. These succulents thrive in a sun-baked position; in shade or if the sun goes in, they close up their flowers. Other sun worshippers that behave in the same way are the daisy-flowered osteospermums, gazanias, arctotis and the Livingstone daisy *(Dorotheanthus bellidiformis* syn. *Mesembryanthemum criniflorum).* The latter would be a good substitute for the portulaca, with its drought-resistant fleshy leaves and low, trailing habit. Deadhead it regularly, otherwise the plants go to seed and stop flowering. Portulacas tend to be sold in midsummer as mature plants in flower. Pots often contain a blend of different shades, which gives a very rich effect. The flowers are grouped in tight clusters at the shoot tips. It is quite difficult to remove spent flowers individually without damaging the buds, so wait until the whole cluster has flowered and then cut the stem back to a side shoot. Take care not to overwater succulent plants such as these; it is better to let them dry out slightly between waterings than to keep them constantly moist. For this reason, if you want to mix portulacas with other foliage, choose similarly drought-resistant types, including helichrysum, *Senecio cineraria*, sedum, sempervivum, *Festuca glauca*, geraniums, *Plecostachys* and *Lotus berthelotii*.

Fitting in plants

If you squeeze the rootball of a potgrown plant into a flattened oval without damaging the roots, you can pack more plants into the same space and achieve a greater concentration of color. Give the plants a good soaking.

1 *Ensure adequate drainage by filling the base of the pot with gravel. This also helps to prevent the drainage hole from clogging with soil.*

2 *Use a soil-based potting mix with extra grit if necessary. Peat-based types do not drain as freely and if they dry out, are very difficult to rewet.*

3 *Try the first plant in the pot and adjust the soil level as necessary. Tilt the rootball slightly so that the arching stems hang over the side of the pot to create a pleasing shape.*

Portulaca grandiflora

4 Add the central plant, again tilting it so that the stems hang down over the front of the pot. Leave room at the back for another plant to go in.

6 Add the final plant at the back of the pot and fill any remaining gaps with soil. Hang the pot where it will receive sunshine for most of the day.

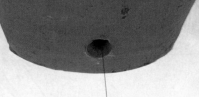

Make sure that wall pots, especially glazed ones, have adequate drainage, as excess moisture cannot escape through the sides as it does in plain terracotta.

5 Balance the shape of the wall basket by adding a third plant on the left-hand side.

Grass and succulents in a terracotta wall pot

This simply decorated terracotta wall pot has a strong Mediterranean feel. Planting schemes invariably work best when the flowers and foliage complement the container, and here sunloving succulents and the steely blue grass *Festuca glauca* fit perfectly. There are many different varieties of *Sempervivum* (houseleek) with fleshy rosettes in various colors, from almost white to dark purple-red. They would not normally be considered for basket planting, but at the front of a small pot like this, their architectural form can be properly appreciated. An alternative group of succulents with similar looks are the frost-tender echeverias. *Echeveria secunda* var. *glauca* has beautiful, pale blue-gray leaves and contrasting spikes of yellow and red. Look for it in the houseplant section of your garden center. Flaming Katy *(Kalanchoe)* is another houseplant that is perfectly happy outdoors during the summer months once hardened off. As well as the usual orange, it is now available in shades of red, pink, yellow and white. The flower display will not last as long as traditional bedding plants, so when it is finished, replace it with other flowering succulents, such as the vibrant portulacas.

4 Plant the houseleek at the front, tilting it slightly so that you can see the rosette clearly. Offsets will grow in due course and trail over the edge.

1 Cover the hole in the base with a flat stone or crock to prevent soil being washed out. Leave the pot unlined for greater drainage.

2 A soil-based potting mixture suits succulents well and, in the event of drying out, is easier to rewet. Fill the base and check the depth as usual.

3 The blue-leaved fescues provide excellent foliage contrast in baskets. They combine especially well with brilliantly colored flowers - yellows, oranges and hot reds. Being hardy and evergreen, they are also suitable for winter interest baskets; transfer them in the fall.

Festuca glauca
(fescue)

Kalanchoe blossfeldiana
(flaming Katy)

5 *Plant the first of the kalanchoes at the back of the basket, filling in the space between the grass and the houseleek with extra soil.*

Sempervivum
'Feldmaier'
(houseleek)

7 *Hook the wall pot onto two screws fixed in a bright position but out of strong midday sun, otherwise the kalanchoe flowers fade too rapidly.*

6 *Add the remaining kalanchoe, tilting it out to the side slightly to balance the shape of the basket. Alternatively, use the succulent trailer Sedum lineare 'Variegatum'.*

A cascade of white and gold

This dark green plastic wall trough makes an excellent foil for the bright lime-colored trails of creeping Jenny (*Lysimachia*) and the bushy spiraea in the center. Overall, the color scheming is quite subtle, but on a white wall, the result is cool, leafy luxuriance. The delicate white-flowered trailer, usually sold under the name *Bacopa*, is set to become an immensely popular basket and container plant. Its correct name is *Sutera cordata* 'Snowflake'. Because of its compact growth and profusion of tiny white flowers, it is an excellent 'filler' for baskets, but also makes a stunning display when planted on its own, its stems growing down to cover the basket sides completely. Trough-like wall baskets lend themselves to symmetrical planting. In a relatively short basket such as this you only need one specimen plant as a centerpiece. The pink-red flowers of the spiraea provide quite a long display, but it is the bright leaf color contrasting with the bronze-tinted new growth that is the main attraction. If you keep it well fed and watered, this basket will continue to look fresh right through into the fall, at which point the spiraea leaves develop attractive tints. Take cuttings of *Sutera* before the frosts to ensure a supply for next year and plant out the hardy lysimachia and spiraea in the garden in a slightly shaded spot to prevent leaf scorch. Cut the spiraea hard back in the spring to encourage plenty of vigorous, bright new growth.

1 *Puncture the base of the trough for drainage; the spots are usually marked. Add gravel or styrofoam chips to prevent holes from clogging.*

2 *Add multipurpose potting mix, checking the level with the largest plant. Leave space for watering.*

3 *Soak the root-ball and place the spiraea in the center of the trough. Soaking plants is vital, as dry rootballs rarely manage to draw up enough moisture from the surrounding soil once planted.*

4 *Add more potting mix to raise the level around the spiraea, then add pots of the gold-leaved creeping Jenny. This has lemon-yellow flowers in early and midsummer.*

5 Fill the remaining gaps with Sutera. As well as white-flowered plants, the gold foliage in this basket would also look good with blue or purple lobelias, cerise-pink and red fuchsias or *Begonia semperflorens*.

Sutera *thrives in sun or part shade and flowers non-stop all summer.*

6 Provided the basket is fed and watered regularly, it will need little in the way of maintenance. Snip off the dead spiraea heads when flowering has finished and trim plants to shape if they grow out of proportion.

Spiraea japonica 'Magic Carpet'

Sutera cordata 'Snowflake'

Trailing plants

Begonia *x* tuberhybrida *varieties*
Bidens ferulifolia
Convolvulus sabatius
Fuchsia *(trailing varieties)*
Glechoma hederacea 'Variegata'
Hedera helix *varieties*
Helichrysum petiolare
Lamium maculatum
Lobelia *(trailing varieties)*
Lotus berthelotii
Petunia *(e.g. 'Supercascade')*
Pelargonium *(ivy-leaved geranium)*
Scaevola aemula *(e.g. 'Blue Fan')*
Sedum lineare 'Variegatum'
Thunbergia alata
Tropaeolum *(nasturtium)*
Verbena *(trailing varieties)*

Lysimachia nummularia 'Aurea'

65

1 *Lay a sheet of recycled wool liner in the basket and press it into place, folding the fabric as necessary. Trim off the excess with sharp scissors. Flexible liners make a better fit and you can cut through them for planting.*

There are several different types of liner, often made from recycled waste products. Choose dark-colored liners, as they tend to fade into the background when you plant up the basket.

A large display of purple and yellow

The daisylike heads of *Asteriscus maritimus* create a splash of gold at the center of this basket. It is in fact a rock garden plant, normally sold under the name 'Gold Coin', but with its dense spreading habit, attractive, round-ended leaves and profusion of flowers, it makes an excellent basket plant, too. Containers planted solely with *Asteriscus* look very effective. Another 'new' plant in this scheme is *Verbena* 'Homestead Purple', a vigorous American cultivar, with wiry stems ending in large, vivid purple flower heads that contrast perfectly with the yellow and gold plants. The basket sides are camouflaged by a yellow-variegated trailing ivy. Ivy is an indispensable basket plant - tough, tolerant and available in a bewildering variety of leaf shapes and variegation. Small specimens, little more than rooted cuttings at the start of summer, rapidly grow into good-sized plants for instant effect in winter and spring baskets. Another plant to salvage from this basket and use as a center-piece for a winter arrangement is *Erica arborea* 'Albert's Gold', whose feathery foliage adds textural interest as well as color.

2 *Add potting mix. As this is a 16in (40cm) basket, use a soilless type, so that it does not get too heavy. Offer up a plant to check the depth.*

3 *Plant yellow-variegated trailing ivy in the top to cover the front and sides of the basket. Vinca minor 'Variegata' would also work.*

4 *Arrange some plants of Asteriscus so that the stems hang over the ivy and create a ring of flowers. Deadhead as flowers turn brown in the center.*

5 *Plant a young specimen of Erica arborea 'Albert's Gold' in the center. Do not worry about providing acid conditions; unlike many heathers, E. arborea grows on lime-rich soils in the wild.*

Erica arborea *'Albert's Gold'*
(tree heath)

Verbena
'Homestead Purple'

6 *Fill the space at the back with purple-flowered verbena, arranging the stems so that some trail forwards and intermingle with the Asteriscus. Dead-head to encourage further blooms.*

Asteriscus maritimus
syn. A. *'Gold Coin'*

Hedera helix *cultivar (variegated ivy)*

7 *Fill in any gaps with potting mix and water well. Allow to drain and hang in a sunny position. Use the correct bracket for this heavy basket.*

A subtropical hanging basket

The brilliant blooms of the Brazilian scarlet sage *(Salvia splendens)* give an exotic, subtropical feel to this basket of lush foliage plants. Foliage is not often considered bold enough to act as much more than a foil for flowers, but here plants such as the multicolored *Houttuynia* and gold-striped sedge take center stage. The *Houttuynia* used in this basket is *H. cordata* 'Chameleon', which needs a well-lit position to develop its coloring properly. During summer, small white flowers with a domed center sometimes appear. The variegated sedge, *Carex hachijoensis* 'Evergold', is another plant that is easy to please, provided its roots do not run short of water. The stiff, grassy foliage arching over the basket sides contrasts perfectly with the broader-leaved *Houttuynia* and *Salvia*. At the end of summer save the carex for a winter basket or plant it at the front of a border in sun or shade to add sparkle to a planting of other winter evergreens. As a dramatic black-leaved alternative to the sedge, you could use another Japanese plant, the evergreen *Ophiopogon planiscapus* 'Nigrescens'. The final element in this basket is a bronze-purple form of bugle, *Ajuga reptans* 'Atropurpurea'. Bugles are normally evergreen to semi-evergreen, depending on the variety and severity of the winter. For the most reliable purple foliage, suitable for covering the sides of a winter basket, choose the cultivar 'Braunherz'. Blue flower spikes normally appear in spring, but bonus flowers often develop later in the year. Ajugas dislike very dry conditions and grow more rapidly when watered freely.

1 *Cut a circle from an old potting mix bag and place it black-side-down in the bottom of the basket to act as a small reservoir so that the roots can still reach moisture between waterings. Camouflage the sides by lifting the plastic and packing sphagnum moss in underneath.*

2 *Fill the reservoir with a moisture-retentive potting mix. Continue to build up the sides of the basket with a thick lining of well-compacted sphagnum moss and add soil to raise the level to planting height.*

3 *Plant three salvias at the back of the basket. The scarlet bracts remain colorful long after the protruding flowers have faded, but once the main spike has gone over, remove it to make way for the shorter flowering side shoots.*

Salvia splendens
(scarlet sage)

Houttuynia cordata
'*Chameleon*'

Ajuga reptans
'*Atropurpurea*'
(purple-leaved bugle)

Carex hachijoensis
'*Evergold*'
(variegated sedge)

4 *Add a couple of trailing, purple-leaved bugles to cover one side of the basket. You could also plant smaller plants between the bars.*

7 *Mulch the top of the basket with a thick layer of sphagnum moss and stand it in a sheltered spot out of direct sun for a few days to allow the plants to settle in. Then hang in full sun.*

5 *Plant the variegated sedge on the opposite side, leaving room in the middle for the Houttuynia. Soak the rootball in a bucket of water and remove any dead or damaged leaves with a pair of nail scissors before planting.*

6 *Add the final plant, tilting it slightly to display the variegated foliage. Squeeze the rootball to fit it in. Fill any gaps between plants with potting mix and add more soil if necessary to fill spaces that appear after watering.*

A late-season pastel display

You can plant virtually anything in a hanging basket: this arrangement uses a mixture of tender bedding plants and hardy shrubs. Baskets are traditionally made up in spring with planting that will last through the whole summer, but that restricts the range of plants that you can use and does not allow for any seasonal variation. Hypericums and hebes are two mainstays of the late summer and fall border and there are compact varieties that also make good temporary subjects for baskets. Low-growing *Hypericum* x *moserianum* 'Tricolor' is a good choice for the front, with its arching stems covered with prettily variegated foliage and buttercup-like flowers. *Hebe* 'Purple Pixie' is just one of a range of small-leaved hebes that flower during summer and fall. Compared with traditional bedding plants, its flowering season is relatively short. For a longer-lasting display, choose *Hebe* 'Autumn Glory' or 'Midsummer Beauty'. Other alternatives for the back of the basket include the blue-flowered *Caryopteris* x *clandonensis* or *Ceratostigma willmottianum*, pinky white *Abelia grandiflora*, fuchsias and bedding dahlias. For fall color at the front, try dwarf Michaelmas daisies (available potgrown from garden centers in late summer), heathers (*Calluna* and *Erica* cultivars) or the creeping *Ceratostigma plumbaginoides*.

Hidden water reservoir below the planting space.

1 Self-watering hanging baskets all have a reservoir, so they do not need daily watering. Here, water is transported to the plant via a wick of capillary matting.

2 Assemble the self-watering basket according to the instructions and stand it in the top of a large, heavy plant pot for stability. Cover the base with potting mix.

3 Offer up the largest plant to check the soil level. There is no watering tube in this basket; excess water drains through to the reservoir for reuse.

4 When planting up just one side of a basket or adding a single large plant, you may find that the basket tips over. To keep it stable and level, counterbalance the weight using a half brick or stone.

5 Arrange the trailing sedum to hang over the right side of the basket and plant the variegated hypericum on the opposite side. Add extra sedums to fill in any gaps.

Hebe 'Purple Pixie'

Begonia semperflorens

Hypericum *x* moserianum 'Tricolor'

Sedum lineare 'Variegatum'

6 White Begonia semperflorens make a visual link between the sedum and hypericum and bridge the height gap between the front and rear.

7 This combination of gentle colors complements the pale, stone-colored basket. Hang it in a well-lit spot, sheltered from the midday sun.

Fitting a large plant into a basket

When you tip a new plant out of its pot, you may find loose soil at the base. Before planting, shake or gently tease the excess away from the roots so that they will fit in a relatively shallow basket.

Dahlias in a wicker basket

This rustic wicker basket, with its soft orange and bronzy-purple coloring, has a distinctly autumnal feel. It overflows with the charming annual climber *Thunbergia alata*, commonly known as black-eyed Susan. This is very easy to raise from seed in spring and much less expensive than buying plants in flower during summer. The stems sometimes become a little congested, so some judicious thinning may be called for to emphasize the elegant trailing habit. Pick up the *Thunbergia* first and carry it around the garden center so that you can match the flower shade exactly with a pot of bedding dahlias. In late summer, garden centers are full of these plants, with their showy blooms in a wide range of colors. Bedding dahlias remain short and compact, and with a flowering period that extends well into the fall, are ideal for container planting. Before adding them to the basket, check plants carefully for slugs and earwigs. Like *Thunbergia*, dahlias need regular feeding and must not be allowed to dry out. Take off the dead flower heads as soon as they fade, as they are quite difficult to distinguish from the buds once the petals have fallen. The glossy bronze-purple foliage of the bugle *Ajuga reptans* 'Atropurpurea' makes a striking contrast with the paler *Thunbergia*, and the trailing foliage rosettes soften the sides of the basket. The more upright *Euphorbia* provides a lighter texture altogether and makes an attractive 'filler'. This is a relatively recent introduction named 'Chameleon'.

1 Line the basket with a black plastic liner. Add some gravel or styrofoam chips to provide a drainage reservoir at the base.

2 Fill the base of the basket with moistened peat-based potting mixture. Firm lightly and then offer up the first plant to see if the level is right.

3 When using plants that have filled their pots with roots, it is especially important to soak the rootball thoroughly before planting it. Submerge it in a bucket and wait until the stream of air bubbles stops.

4 You may need to weigh down the opposite side of the basket to stop it tipping over while you decide where to plant the dahlia.

Euphorbia dulcis 'Chameleon'.
The bracts develop paler
red and pink tints
in the fall.

Dahlia
'Dahlietta
Apricot'
(bedding
dahlia)

5 Lift up the dahlia foliage
and tuck the Ajuga in
underneath, arranging the
trails so that they fall over
the edge of the basket.

6 Add a couple of pots of Euphorbia
between the dahlia and black-eyed
Susan. Take care, as all euphorbias exude
a milky-white irritant sap if damaged.

Ajuga reptans
'Atropurpurea'

7 Complete the basket with
more ajugas and fill in
round the plants with potting
mix. Hang it up in a position
out of extreme midday sun,
which would bleach the
flowers. To complement the
coloring, use a gold chain
attached to the hanging hoop.

Thunbergia alata
(black-eyed Susan)

73

Violas and ivy with a fuchsia for foliage

In the border, you can enhance the beauty of individual flowering plants with a suitable backdrop of foliage. Here, the same principle has been applied to highlight a mass of viola blooms. Bedding violas are available in a range of shades, including plain and bicolored varieties. Some are almost black and tend to 'disappear' in a mixed arrangement. This velvet purple variety with its paler lilac center is much more visible, but still needs to be surrounded by lighter foliage to do it justice. White variegated plants complement the flowers perfectly. The elegant fuchsia variety 'Sharpitor' used at the back of the basket is quite unlike most bedding varieties. It has very pale green leaves, edged creamy white, with slender pendent flowers of blush pink, which are most profuse in the fall. As it is frost hardy you can replant it in the border when you dismantle the display. Variegated ground ivy and real ivy provide a foil at the front. For a brighter overall effect, try lime green and gold-variegated foliage, including the gold-leaved fuchsia variety 'Genii', *Helichrysum* 'Limelight', *Salvia officinalis* 'Icterina', golden feverfew *(Tanacetum parthenium* 'Aureum', and for trails, golden creeping Jenny (see page 64) and gold-variegated ivy.

4 Soak the remaining plants before use. Add the fuchsia specimen at the back of the basket. Plant the first of the violas, leaving room for the ground ivy.

3 Separate a pot of rooted ivy cuttings and plant some between the basket wires. Pack moss around the necks to prevent drying out and loss of soil.

1 Cut a circle of black plastic from an old potting mix bag and use it to line the base of the basket. Camouflage the edges with sphagnum moss.

2 The plastic lining traps moisture and acts like a small reservoir for the plants to draw on. Fill the basket with potting mix and add more moss.

Support the basket on a pot while you work to keep it steady.

74

Fuchsia magellanica
molinae *'Sharpitor'*
*(variegated hardy
fuchsia)*

Bedding violas

7 *Keep all the
plants well
watered and hang
the basket in a spot
out of the midday
sun to keep the
arrangement cool.
Few bedding plants
need full sun and a
little shade often
helps the blooms
to last longer.*

5 *Add trailing ground ivy
around the edge to
mingle with the ivy trails.
Ground ivy roots easily;
once you have one plant, you
should never need another!*

6 *Add the remaining
violas and fill any gaps
with potting mix. The
violas will sort themselves
out over the next few days.
Deadhead them regularly .*

Glechoma hederacea
'Variegata'
(variegated ground ivy)

Hedera helix *'Mini Adam'*
(variegated ivy)

75

An ivy chicken basket

Planted with moss and ivy and hung by the front door, this chicken basket is sure to attract attention! Ivies with extra-small leaves are a good choice for this arrangement, as they make a dense evergreen covering without obscuring the detail of the container. The basket demonstrates a simple but very effective technique that you can apply to make other hanging shapes, including spheres, which are made by joining two ordinary wire hanging baskets together. You can either plant in the top of the basket and train foliage to cover the outside as shown here, or using small rooted cuttings, plant directly through the sides. Baskets made in this way are more tricky to keep, especially during very hot weather, as you really need to keep the moss moist if the exposed extremities are to remain green. The easiest method is to soak the basket by sitting the base in a bowl of water. The sphagnum moss acts like a wick and draws water up through the shape. You should also add water as normal in the top of the basket to ensure that the potting mixture remains moist at all times. If the arrangement is growing indoors or in a conservatory, mist spray it daily to keep it looking its best for as long as possible.

2 *Stuff the head with moist, tightly packed sphagnum moss that will remain in position even if it shrinks slightly. Line the rest of the basket with a thick layer of well-compressed moss, leaving a hollow planting center.*

3 *Fill the center with a moisture-retentive, hanging basket potting mixture. Work it thoroughly into the interior space and firm it down gently.*

1 *This unusual wire basket is actually an egg-holder bought from a kitchen equipment store. The black plastic coating really makes it stand out and also prevents rusting. The ivy variety 'Mini Adam' was chosen because of the feathery appearance of the pointed, white-edged leaves.*

Hedera helix 'Mini Adam'

4 *Divide up the pots of ivy, separating out the individual cuttings. Plant them in the top of the basket, making a hole for each root clump with your fingers. Arrange them in a circle for even coverage when trained.*

Choose pots of ivy with long trails for quick coverage.

5 *Cut lengths of florist's wire into halves or thirds and bend them like hairpins. Cover the moss-filled body with ivy by pinning the trails at intervals.*

6 *Leave the head uncovered so that the detail is still visible. Add some extra ivy trails to emphasize the tail, hooking them through the frame.*

Loose ivy trails arch down to make the tail feathers.

7 *Attach a handle of fine chain to the basket so that you can hang it up using a butcher's hook. Adjust the position so that it hangs level.*

1 *Turn the basket upside down and if there are no guidance marks, pinpoint the position of your drainage holes with a soft pencil or felt-tip pen. Drill holes carefully through the plastic base.*

A large winter display

The delicate combination of foliage and flower is just right for this classical basket. Its pale blue-green coloring is reminiscent of ice, so the planting is designed to create a frosted effect. You could choose all-white plants, but the gradation of white through to pink is even more effective. Ornamental cabbages and cut-leaved kales produce a central rosette of foliage that is either rich purple, pink, white or a combination of these colors. Here, a deep pink cabbage highlights the much paler, frilly-leaved one at the front. These cabbages tend to lose their outer leaves through the winter, but usually produce new growth at the center. Remove yellowing leaves with sharp scissors. Erratic watering and changes in the weather can cause the plants to bolt (flower prematurely), which looks rather odd as the center telescopes out. If this happens, replace them with something equally bold, say a dwarf pink-flowered bergenia, such as 'Baby Doll'. Female varieties of the evergreen *Gaultheria* are smothered with marble-like berries by mid-fall and the fruits usually last well into late winter. An ordinary peat-based potting mixture suits these ericaceous (lime-hating) plants well. Weather-resistant, winter-flowering heathers, usually varieties of *Erica carnea*, are ideal for winter baskets, flowering for several months.

4 *Plant the largest element - here a Gaultheria mucronata - at the back. Add the heather, arranging the shoots to soften the basket edge.*

2 *Break styrofoam seed trays into chips as a lightweight substitute for gravel drainage. Fill the tapering base of this large basket completely, otherwise it will weigh too much.*

3 *Cover the styrofoam pieces with potting mixture. Check that there is enough room for the largest of the plant rootballs, allowing space at the top for watering. Lightly firm the soil.*

Ornamental
cabbage

Gaultheria mucronata
(formerly Pernettya
mucronata*)* 'White Pearl'

Erica carnea
'Springwood White'
(heather)

5 *Put in the ornamental cabbages opposite the heather, leaving a gap in the center for the pansies. Tilt the heads slightly to show off the centers.*

Pansy
Ultima series
'Pink Shades' F1

6 *Fill the center with a selection of pansies of subtly different shades to draw all the elements of the basket together. Fill the gaps with soil.*

Ornamental cabbage

7 *Water and allow to drain before attaching the three chains to the basket rim. Hang in a sunny spot sheltered from wind. Water only when the soil surface dries out slightly.*

79

1 *Cut a circle of plastic from an old potting mixture bag and use it black-side-down to line the base of a wire basket.*

2 *Add some potting mix to act as a small reservoir that helps to prevent water from draining away too rapidly.*

A cheerful basket of evergreens

This cheerful basket will liven up even the darkest winter day. The scarlet primroses really sparkle and their bold yellow centers are accentuated by the golden-variegated euonymus. From the fall to early winter, you should find all the necessary ingredients for this basket at garden centers; many young shrubs in small pots are available at this time. They may seem quite expensive for a seasonal basket, but you can of course plant them out in the garden once the display is over. Instead of the golden euonymus, you could try its white-variegated counterpart 'Emerald Gaiety', evergreen herbs and hebes, such as the pink-flushed 'Red Edge' or silver-leaved *Hebe pinguifolia* 'Pagei'. Although more often associated with summer bedding displays, cineraria is reasonably hardy and it is worth potting up a few plants towards the end of summer. Cut back any long straggly shoots or flower stems to promote bushy new growth and keep them in a sunny spot for use later on. You can always find pots of ivy with long trails in the houseplant section of garden centers; outdoor ones are rarely so luxuriant. Gradually introduce the ivy to outdoor conditions and temperatures before planting it. Conifer hedge clippings make a good substitute for moss in baskets. The fresh green coloring is especially welcome in winter - it lasts for months without turning brown. Use it thickly to help insulate the basket and prevent the soil from freezing.

Pliable, leafy, conifer hedge clippings make an excellent basket lining.

3 *Build up the conifer lining inside the basket, tucking the foliage under the edge of the plastic circle. Weave the pieces into each other and through the basket bars.*

4 *Add more potting mix until you reach the point where the first plant is to go in. Offer up the euonymus and adjust the soil level.*

5 Plant the euonymus through the bars. Place the rootball on the potting mix and feed the stems through; they are tough and pliable.

6 Continue to build up the conifer lining, adding more potting mix. Plant the silver cineraria in the top of the basket.

7 Plant scarlet-red hybrid primroses as the centerpiece, with one tilted over the edge to show off its flowers. Add another euonymus at the back as a foil for the flowers.

8 Add a well-grown pot of trailing ivy to balance the design. Fill in all the gaps between the plants. Water in thoroughly and allow to drain.

Senecio cineraria 'Silver Dust'

Hybrid primroses

Euonymus fortunei 'Emerald 'n' Gold'

Hedera helix 'Ester'

9 Hang the basket in a sheltered spot outdoors, say from a hook fixed under the overhang of an open porch. Water only when the surface of the potting mixture starts to dry out.

Eye-catching pots of gold

The life of primroses can easily be extended, especially if you choose good plants in the first place. Look for compact primroses with many buds still to come and healthy, stiff dark green leaves. Gently tip the plant out of its pot to look at the root system, which should be white and well developed. Avoid plants that are pale and drawn, as these will have been kept too warm with insufficient light. Overwatering is a common problem, too. It is best to leave watering until the foliage has just started to go limp. Avoid overhead watering as this marks the foliage and flowers. Provided the basket is protected from the elements, it can be reused time and again. After the primroses, you could continue the gold theme with dwarf daffodils or little yellow violas and replace these later on with *Calceolaria* 'Sunshine' or a yellow *Kalanchoe* (flaming Katy).

1 A simple color scheme - butter-yellow primroses and a gold chain - picks out the unusual detailing on this delightful wicker basket.

2 Make the basket waterproof by lining it with plastic. You can cut a circle of the appropriate size from a black bag, as here. Press the pleated lining into position inside the basket.

3 Carefully trim off any excess plastic until it is just below the rim of the basket so that it will be hidden by the soil. Black or clear plastic is the easiest to camouflage.

Hardy primroses

Throughout the winter period, garden centers have tempting trays of brightly colored primroses for sale. These are normally already in flower, which makes color scheming your baskets much easier. However, be careful when buying as they are not all frost hardy - check the label or ask an assistant. Seed catalogues now offer several weather-resistant varieties, so you could grow your own supply. If you plan to grow primroses indoors, keep them in a cool, well-lit position.

8 *Hang the basket in a sheltered spot. The gold chain complements the basket and the hook is made from the opened-out link of a larger chain.*

4 *Add a layer of gravel to provide a drainage reservoir in the base. This helps prevent overwatering, which can cause leaves to turn yellow and rot.*

5 *Cover the gravel with soil- or peat-based potting mixture and then test the depth by popping in one of the primroses to see the effect.*

Some leaves will turn yellow as a matter of course. Remove them at the base with a pair of sharp nail scissors, along with any faded blooms.

6 *Plant the primroses, arranging the foliage to fit around the handle and drape over the edge. Cut off any leaves that are squashed together at the center of the arrangement.*

7 *Fill the gaps in between plants with more potting mixture. Firm the soil gently, making sure that there are no air pockets, as these prevent the plant roots from developing. Settle the soil in by watering, but do not overwater.*

1 Cut a piece of plastic sheeting to line the back of the basket and protect the wall. One corner of an empty potting mixture bag is ideal. Turn the plastic up at the base to form a lip. It may help to plant the basket in its final position to keep it stable as you work.

2 Line the front and sides of the basket with some sphagnum moss. If necessary, you can use moss salvaged from summer baskets. Use a thick, tightly packed layer to act as insulation and to prevent soil from seeping out.

3 Add potting mixture to fill the base of the basket to just below the level of moss shown in the photograph. Break up pots of rooted ivy cuttings into manageable chunks ready for planting through the bars of the wall basket.

A winter wall basket with berries

The festive-looking winter cherry arrives in the shops during late fall and makes an ideal subject for a basket by the front door over the holiday period. Here, pure white cyclamen, again readily available at this time of year, and white-variegated ivy provide a foil for the orange-red berries. For a richer combination, you could try scarlet-red cyclamen and dark green ivy. Although these varieties are traditionally thought of as houseplants, they will grow outdoors provided they have a sheltered, frost-free position; the warmth given out from the walls of a house and shelter from an overhead porch may be sufficient in areas where the winter is relatively mild or in the inner city.

When buying winter cherries, look for bushy plants, well-clothed in dark green leaves. There should be plenty of mostly still unripe, green berries; these will eventually turn orange. Plants like this will provide color right through until late winter.

4 Guide the trails of ivy carefully through the bars, resting the rootball on top of the soil. This arrangement uses four pots of ivy.

5 Pack in more sphagnum moss around the neck of each clump of ivy and then continue to build up the moss lining until it reaches the top of the basket. Plant two winter cherries towards the back of the basket, leaving a gap at the front.

6 When planting the cyclamen, tilt it slightly forward so that the handsome marbled foliage hangs over the edge of the basket. Tilting the plant also helps to prevent water from collecting in the crown, which could cause the cyclamen to rot.

Solanum pseudocapsicum *'Thurino'*

Cyclamen persicum

Maintenance

The plants in this basket have slightly different watering requirements. The rootball of the winter cherry should be kept constantly moist, otherwise the berries tend to drop prematurely. Ivy is quite drought-tolerant and cyclamen should be allowed to dry out slightly between waterings to prevent rotting. Do not water overhead; instead, use a watering can with a long narrow spout so that you can target the amount more accurately. Remove faded cyclamen flowers, along with any dead or yellowing leaves, with a pair of sharp nail scissors.

Hedera helix *'Hvid Kolibri'*

Hedera helix *'Adam'*

7 Fill the gaps between plants with more soil and cover the surface with moss to prevent erosion when watering. Water thoroughly and allow to drain.

A basket of pansies

Wicker baskets are available in all shapes and sizes. Most are unlined, but lining them is a very simple process. Since wicker is best kept under cover to prevent weathering, a wicker basket makes an ideal container for winter bedding. This also relishes the protection of an open or enclosed porch, unheated conservatory or sunroom, as it can suffer if the potting mixture freezes or when exposed to cold winds. The most widely sold winter-flowering pansies are the weather-resistant Universal and Ultima series. Most pansies can be made to flower throughout the year by sowing them at different times, so do not be surprised to see summer bedding varieties on sale in winter. As plants put on little growth until spring, choose bushy specimens with healthy dark green foliage and plenty of flower buds. Plants that show no signs of flowering are unlikely to produce blooms until spring. A basket edged in ivy can be planted up with all kinds of flowering plants, including double daisies, hybrid primroses and even dwarf bulbs, provided the container is deep enough. Keep them in a cool but sheltered place, such as a cold frame, until the bulbs are just starting to show flower buds and then bring them out on display. If you forget to buy bulbs in the fall, garden centers have a selection in pots for instant planting from midwinter.

3 *Cover the pebbles with potting mix, making sure that there is still room for the pansies and ivy on top. Check the level with a plant and adjust as necessary.*

1 *Containers with a handle convert easily to hanging baskets. This wicker basket was bought ready-lined and is ideal for use indoors, where drips may be a problem.*

2 *The sealed lining protects the basket from discoloration, but plants may become waterlogged. Add a layer of pebbles or similar material as a drainage reservoir.*

Hedera helix
'Mint Kolibri'
(ivy)

Pansy Crystal Bowl Series
'Sky Blue' F1

Add just enough water to settle the soil around the plants. Add more soil if gaps appear. Thereafter, water sparingly, allowing the soil surface to dry out slightly between waterings.

Pack the plants in tightly for maximum impact.

4 Make a continuous edging of foliage by splitting the ivy (see panel). Arrange the long trails to hang over the edges. You could also wind some pieces around the handle.

5 Plant the pansies close together in the center of the basket; they will not grow much during the winter. Fill the spaces in between with potting mix and firm in.

6 Hang the basket by a homemade rope fixed around the handle. Disguise the join with raffia. If you prefer, use a large hook and chain.

Dividing ivy

Each pot of trailing ivy probably contains seven or eight rooted cuttings around the rim. For this basket edging, simply open out the circle of cuttings into a straight line. Ivy roots easily; you can produce a winter supply by propagating it in summer. It is also available all year from garden centers.

Ferns in an oriental basket

The container you select will often dictate the type of foliage and flowers you choose to plant in it. This little basket looks very similar to the bamboo pots used in Chinese cooking, so a plant with an oriental feel was chosen to fill it. The foliage of the *Pteris* fern looks at first glance like that of dwarf bamboo and the pale biscuit color of the basket shows off the rich green fronds perfectly. *Pteris* ferns are some of the easiest to maintain and tolerate temperatures as low as 45°F(7°C) in winter. Like all ferns they enjoy a humid atmosphere, so hang them in the bathroom or near the kitchen sink and try to remember to mist the foliage daily with tepid water. They are ideal for brightening up a window that receives no sun at midday or for hanging in the shaded end of a conservatory. Indeed, you must keep *Pteris* out of direct sunlight otherwise the leaves may scorch. The success of this basket demonstrates the fact that you do not need a variety of plants to make a good display. Simplicity is nearly always the key to success. If you can, try to imagine your proposed plantings in black and white so that you are able to concentrate on the form of the foliage and flower as opposed to the color. That way, you can see if there is enough textural interest and overall contrast between the different elements. In the basket described here, the leaves of the fern have such a beautiful shape and shading, that there is really no need to introduce another variety.

Indoor plants with an oriental flavor

Aeschynanthus radicans *(lipstick vine)*, Asparagus ferns
Foliage begonias, such as Begonia rex *hybrids*
Forest cacti (Schlumbergera and Rhipsalidopsis)
Clerodendrum thomsoniae
Red mini-cyclamen
Columnea *sp. (goldfish plant and varieties)*
Dwarf Cyperus *(keep moist)*
Euonymus japonicus 'Aureus'
Ficus radicans 'Variegata'
Red, single-flowered, trailing fuchsia, e.g. 'Marinka'
Lachenalia aloides
Maranta leuconeura erythroneura *(herringbone plant)*
Scirpus cernuus *(keep moist)*

1 *Add gravel to provide a layer of drainage in the base of the container. This basket is ready lined and has no drainage holes.*

2 *Cover the gravel with a peat-based potting mix. At this stage you can offer up a plant to check the depth and ensure that there will be a sufficient gap at the top to allow for watering.*

88

Pteris cretica albolineata *(variegated table fern)*

3 *Before putting in any plants, soak the rootballs thoroughly. Put in the first of the three Pteris ferns. Odd numbers work better than even ones.*

The basket is made of thin strips of wood, not bamboo, and has a wooden handle.

6 *Suspend the basket using natural colored twine or raffia to blend in with the other materials. If hung over a kitchen work surface, you could use a butchers hook and length of chain.*

4 *Add the remaining ferns, adjusting their position so that the foliage fills the basket and works in comfortably around the handle.*

Keep plants looking their best by removing brown or damaged fronds at the base with nail scissors. Take care not to damage the new shoots growing up from the base.

5 *Fill the gaps in between with more potting mix and firm in. Water to settle the soil. Ferns like a constantly moist but not wet soil, so take care not to overwater this sealed container.*

Index to Plants

Page numbers in **bold** indicate major text references. Page numbers in *italics* indicate captions and annotations to photographs. Other text entries are shown in normal type.

Credits

The majority of the photographs featured in this book have been taken by Neil Sutherland and are © Colour Library Books. The publishers wish to thank the following photographers for providing additional photographs, credited here by page number and position on the page, i.e. (B)Bottom, (T)Top, (C)Center, (BL)Bottom left, etc.

Eric Crichton: 21(B)

John Glover: Half-title, 8, 12(L,BR), 13(TL,BL), 18(TR,BC), 19(L,R), 20(T,B), 21(TL,TR)

Acknowledgments

The publishers would like to thank Grosvenor Garden Centre, Belgrave, Chester and Bridgemere Garden World, Nantwich, Cheshire for supplying plants and containers for photography.